Promises, Promises

Promises, Promises

By

Onedia N. Gage

Other Books by Onedia N. Gage

As We Grow Together Daily Devotional for Expectant Couples

As We Grow Together Prayer Journal for Expectant Couples

The Blue Print: Poetry for the Soul

In Purple Ink: Poetry for the Spirit

Living An Authentic Life

The Measure of a Woman: The Details of Her Soul

On This Journey Daily Devotional for Young People

On This Journey Prayer Journal for Young People

Promises, Promises

Yielded and Submitted: A Woman's Journey Back to God

PROMISES, PROMISES

All Rights Reserved © 2001 by Onedia N. Gage

No part of this book may be reproduced or transmitted in any form or by any means, graphic, electronic, or mechanical, including photocopying, recording, taping, or by any information storage retrieval system, without the permission in writing from the publisher.

Published by Purpleink, Inc

For information address:

Purpleink, Inc, P O Box 27242, Houston, TX 77227

www.purpleink.net

ISBN: 978-0-9801002-8-0

Printed in the United States of America

I say to myself, "The Lord is my portion; therefore I will wait for him."
Lamentations 3:24 (NIV)

And whatever you do, whether in word or deed, do it all in the name of the Lord Jesus, giving thanks to God the Father through him.
Colossians 3:17 (NIV)

And without faith it is impossible to please God, because anyone who comes to him must believe that he exists and that he rewards those who earnestly seek him.
Hebrews 11:6 (NIV)

Dedication

The late Mr. Joseph Renty: Thank you for defining 'Philip.' Thank you for being my great-grandmother's 'Philip.'

The late Mr. Cornelious C. Carroll: Thank you for being an example of 'Philip.'

Master Nehemiah C. Broussard: I am working on your ability to be a 'Philip.'

Miss Hillary N. Broussard: I am praying for your 'Philip.'

For the late Mrs. Mary Renty: I love and miss you dearly.

Mary, Joseph and Cornelious: I know you are looking down on me and I hope you are proud of what you see.

ACKNOWLEDGEMENTS

To God, the Almighty, Omnipotent, Powerful Presence of Christ as You reside in my heart. Lord, I love You and I thank You for Your gifts and talents. I honor Your excellence and Your goodness.

Andrea Moseley Scott. Andrea, if I write anything about you and don't cry then I didn't write anything. Thank you for your obedience to God. Thank you for your prayers and support and fasting in my place. I love you.

Randy L. Boone: My Prayer Warrior intercedes. Thank you for each prayer on my behalf, in my place. God gives through people whose motives are pure and whose rights are relinquished. Randy, God has definitely given through you. We've seen an awful lot of prayers answered. And many more to come. I'm waiting on my greeting cards.

Special Thanks to Anita Richmond Bunkley, Angela Benson, Norma L. Jarrett and ConSandra Jones.

To my church family, Brookhollow Baptist/The Church Without Walls, who are too many to name, but specifically to my prayer warriors and spiritual leadership: Pastor & Mrs. Ralph Douglas West, The Brookhollow staff, Mr. & Mrs. Willie Brown, Mr. & Mrs. Dempsey Wells, Jr., Mr. & Mrs. Roland Martin, Ms. Reanice Weakley, and the women and the youth of the Brook.

FOREWARD

Dear Friend:

I thank you for reading this book for there were many nights when I thought of who you would be. The nights that I spent up late writing this book have all been made worthwhile because you have your hands on the spine of this book.

I pray that Toni motivates and inspires you to reach for your dreams. I hope that you indulge yourself in her life and pick the parts that are your own. Goals are easily written; harder to see; hardest to believe when intangible. She will warm your heart and become part of your life.

One more word: Finish what you start. Believe that your dreams can come true. Anything worth dreaming about is worth working for. Develop a philosophy for your life and live by it.

I encourage you to reach me at www.purpleink.net or www.onediagage.com. Purple ink originated from a friend asking me did I always write in purple and I said yes. Purple soothes me and calms my soul. I implore you to find your purple ink—the thing that makes you respond with love.

In purpleink,
Onedia N. Gage
onediagage@purpleink.net
onediagage@onediagage.com

Chapter One

"Welcome to the American Association of Doctors—Houston Affiliate's 75th Anniversary Celebration and Awards Gala. Please peruse the history of the organization at your leisure.

"It is my honor to present our master of ceremonies this evening. His list of accolades, achievements, education and philanthropic efforts are listed for your review. I will remind you that he was last year's Randolph Award recipient and the world's leading neurosurgeon. Without further adieu, Dr. Philip Morris." The AAD president met Philip with a handshake.

"That's the best introduction I've ever had and the best one I've heard in awhile." The crowd let out a light-hearted chuckle. Dr. Morris continued, "We are glad to have you as our guests this evening. We are here to celebrate our 75th year as an affiliate and to honor some very special doctors who serve our communities selflessly, as well. These doctors give freely of their time and money to improve the quality of life for others. So, all I ask is that you laugh at just the right moments, you clap on time and you enjoy the evening. We have quite the evening planned for you." The audience laughed again as he charmed them with his wit.

"The gala also raises money for these same doctors to continue their work. So I know you've already bid at the silent auction." He had to chuckle himself. He continued to entertain the crowd with stories of each doctor as he adorned them with their awards.

As he spoke of the other doctors, Toni remembered their first meeting. She had volunteered to do rounds for a vacationing colleague. She went on the day Dr. Morris was responsible for. When they ended up in the same patient's room, she realized her error. She introduced herself as she extended her hand. "Dr. Antoinette Harden. You must be Dr. Morris." She was somewhat taken aback by his meek disposition.

"Yes, but call me Philip. Did I get my days mixed up?" He paused.

"No, I must have. I don't see how I could forget. I'm a day early." She blushed, "I apologize."

He stared at her intently, "That's okay. Better early than late. Originally, I had plans. I can do tomorrow if you want."

"I feel so bad. I promised to help. But sure. I've already seen the ones in the north wing." His intensity caused her to stammer.

"I'll do both days. Dr. Harden, don't worry about it. I'm sure such a busy woman must have other things she could be doing." He realized that she was more attractive than he remembered from the AAD awards ceremony earlier in the year. He received the "Randolph Award" after she gave the keynote speech.

"Thank you, but please call me Toni," she waved goodbye. He disappeared in the other direction.

She remembered wondering about him then. Now he was standing in front of her. She wondered was he still dating his college sweetheart. When she inquired after last year's gala, rumor had it that he was seriously dating his college sweetheart. She made a mental note to inquire again. He was more handsome than she remembered and truly charming.

Dr. Morris captured the audience's heart with his witty anecdotes and comedic demeanor. He sobered for a moment when he introduced Toni.

"Our last award recipient and last year's keynote speaker has quite the résumé for one of such youth. She has a commitment to youth that is unsurpassed by anyone in our field. She said last year in her address that there is worth in each of their fragile lives. This pediatrician serves them with that very commitment. The children she serves trust her and bond with her immediately. Her commitment is measured by the number she serves regularly at the clinic, not her private practice. She has increased the number of youth served by 75%.

"Her most memorable case was a young girl named Tabitha. Tabitha had fallen from the back of a truck while traveling with her brothers to pick pecans to earn money for the family. She is eight years old. She asked if Dr. Harden had ever picked pecans from a tree. Dr. Harden shared a story with her about her great-grandfather and his pecan trees, and about her great-grandmother and her pecan pies.

"Tabitha later asked if Dr. Harden would ever stop helping people who couldn't afford medical care. Dr. Harden told her no. She never would stop. Tabitha smiled. She then went on to say how special Dr. Harden had become to her during her short stay at the hospital. She confessed that she didn't want to go home. Dr. Harden asked why and she started to cry. She said that no one cares for her the way Dr. Harden had. She said that when Dr. Harden hugged her, she felt better, and she was happy. She said no one had ever hugged her like that before. Dr. Harden hugged and held her for long time. She cried until she fell asleep. Dr. Harden credits Tabitha with inspiring her to continue her work, especially when it's hard. Tabitha reminded Dr. Harden that it does take a village to raise a child, and the village doesn't retire. Tabitha then becomes an educated member of the village and will continue to educate and nurture the younger members.

"When I heard that story, I found myself labeling her as the Florence Nightingale of the 21st century. Our honoree is in constant communication with Tabitha and her family." He casually glanced down at Toni. "Our doctor has never been an underachiever. She earned her medical degree from Johns Hopkins School of Medicine, graduating first in her class. With that alone, she was offered intern opportunities at the top medical branches across the country. But she rejected those offers to return to Houston. Dr. Harden used her leverage to write a pilot program proposal where she would complete her internship and residency between two hospitals, Riverside General and Texas Children's Hospitals. The doctor who accepted her proposal later became her mentor. He interviewed her over the phone. As you might guess this is unheard of in this industry. Her proposal prompted several funding sources.

"She started work immediately upon graduation. Because of this pilot program, not only did she become a doctor in record time, she also attained a nationally commendable reputation in the arena of pediatrics. She also received merit as a child advocate. Needless to say her contributions impacted our communities without precedence. Her proposal and the completion of the program aided in the care of 600 more patients each year, and included a state of the art facility and equipment, and $5 million dollars in additional funding over a three year period dedicated to children in need of medical services without health care insurance, without consideration of Medicare and Medicade.

"Dr. Antoinette Harden used the best of both worlds to upgrade the treatment of children everywhere she touched. Just to give a little more depth into the awardees' life, I have a video of last year's keynote address." Philip cued the video and watched her as if it were his first time hearing these words.

"Greetings fellow honorees, colleagues, staff and guests! This evening I am quite inspired. When I first decided to become a physician, instead of an attorney, it was a shock to most. Those who don't know why always seem astonished when I explain that helping children feel better even when they can't explain where it hurts is amazing. Your child can't always tell you where it hurts or what it feels like, but when they come to my office and they leave feeling better, I feel great. For them to feel better with just a simple hug and some attention astonishes me the most.

"My great-grandmother always told me to be somebody. Of course, I didn't realize until I was much older that I didn't know who she wanted me to be. Who was somebody? What made a person become 'somebody'? Then I realized that other children my age had no clue either. We knew who we didn't want to be. All the while, what my great grandmother meant for me to be was somebody with integrity, ethics, values, morals, sensitivity, thoughtfulness, love and a humanitarian nature. She meant for me to respect old people, young people and middle-aged people. She wished for me to hug babies and care for my family. She prayed for me to be Christ-like, honest and kind. She wanted me to love others more than they love me. She instilled in me the values of a human being to peacefully co-exist with other human beings. These are my goals each day. This is what I attempt to show the children each day.

"Children possess instinct. They understand that honesty is a virtue. They know when you're not honest. They also judge character very well. They know who is genuine and who is not. Contrary to adult opinion, they understand more than we would like to admit. They sense when adults are having problems. They understand when adults are happy, too. Where we fail is our attempt to hide what is the reality. Children want you to be real. Mostly, they just want to be loved. They want your attention; special quality time. Television is not quality time. They want you to listen. They want you to hug them. They want a friend, one they can trust. They want your very best. They want all you have and more. They can demand that because they will give all they have.

"Now, what we need is to become a role model, a mentor and help them be 'somebody'. A someone who is a genuine, loving person, an honest, ethical individual that will result in a humanitarian. We have a responsibility to raise these children with the village mentality. We have a responsibility to raise them to be sensible and sensitive, to be thinkers as well as hard workers, to be individualists and team players, to be independent while co-existing in a shared space, to lead and also to follow. We have to teach them to become adults who live by principles as the Bible and Robert Fulghum's *All I Really Needed to Know I Learned in Kindergarten*. These are basic concepts, and these books are not always as readily available. They need to realize that they too will one day encounter the same obstacles that occur to you and me. They simply need to be given the tools to make the best choices.

"Do you remember the little boy in the movie "Jerry McGuire?" He is a classic child model. He was so honest and so real. He was a child and so full of life. He made life appear easy and without pain. He just wanted to be loved and listened to.

"For those of you who have never heard it, and especially for those of you who need reminding, I will read the passage of which I speak: "All I Really Needed to Know" is about how to live and what to do and how to be I learned in kindergarten. Wisdom was not at the top of the graduate school mountain, but there in the sand pile at Sunday school.

These are the things I learned:

Share everything.

Play fair.

Don't hit people.

Put things back where you found them.

Clean up your own mess.

Don't take things that aren't yours.

Say you're sorry when you hurt somebody.

Wash your hands before you eat.

Flush.

Warm cookies and cold milk are good for you.

Live a balanced life—learn some and think some and draw and paint and sing and dance and play and work every day some.

Take a nap every afternoon.

When you go out into the world, watch out for traffic, hold hands, and stick together. Be aware of wonder.
Remember the little seed in the Styrofoam cup: The roots go down and the plant goes up and nobody really knows how or why, but we are all like that.
Goldfish and hamsters and white mice and even the little seed in the Styrofoam cup—they all die.
So do we.
And then remember the Dick-and-Jane books and the first word you learned—the biggest word of all—LOOK."

"I challenge you to keep this in your office and cherish it. If you reflect on the actual times in your life when these things were important, you will embrace your life, your family, your triumphs, your adversities, and all that is surrounding you with a new spirit and a whole new attitude. All we need is to be inspired. All we need is support and encouragement. All we need is to be that to one another. Children have feelings and they have hurt and pain, too. We need to remember that when we communicate. Lastly, I challenge you to hug a child. I challenge you to let their free spirit embrace yours. I challenge you to let all they are seep into your body so you can become what you have forgotten and release that tension and stress. I challenge you to hug a child so long that when the embrace is finally over you have had some self-therapy. I challenge you to be the adult with the spirit of a child. I challenge you to live the words of *All I Really Needed to Know I Learned in Kindergarten*. Thank you."

As they raised the house lights, Philip spoke, "The youngest kid on the block is insuring that all the kids on the block have a chance to make it by giving her time, efforts and money."

"Ladies and gentlemen, I present to you Dr. Antoinette Harden." Dr. Morris reached for a large crystal vase and turned to face Toni. He spoke slowly and deliberately as he explained, "'The Randolph Award' is very special to me because Dr. Randolph presented it to me personally last year.

"Dr. Harden, it is truly a pleasure to bestow this award upon you. You truly deserve it. You make me feel as if like I didn't really earn my award. On a serious note, this award is given to you on behalf of your colleagues and staff for the hard work that you do to influence change for a healthier community. Your commitment to youth is to be preserved and appreciated for there is worth in each of their fragile lives. You have recognized this and turned our community into a health-conscious one. This vase is a simple token of our gratitude for your commitment and dedication. We hope that you will remember why your efforts are significant when you look at it. And you already have something to put in it." He gestured to the roses at the end of the stage. "Dr. Antoinette Harden, congratulations."

Toni heard the thunderous applause and couldn't believe it was for her. With streaming tears, she embraced her gifts. She approached the podium with reverence, "You never know what you've done until you hear others say it. Dr. Morris, thank you for that introduction and those very warm words. The video was quite surprising. As colleagues, thank you for your confidence in me and my work. The people that I need, and want, to thank is endless so I will do that last. My job is important, and I'm not the one who makes it so. The children do. They make it important, worthwhile, fulfilling and rewarding.

"I am proud to announce my promotion in this village to educator and nurturer. Again, I felt the love and honesty that little people have for adults who assist them in their endeavors. I needed to feel assurance from a child that my work was beneficial and worthwhile. I decided then to increase my commitment and the care that is provided to young ones just like Tabitha. Tabitha will forever be special to me. She has since left the hospital, but has been given some very special follow-up care. I accept this award in honor of Tabitha. Now I have two things to remind me of my commitment: this beautiful vase and my images of Tabitha.

"There are some people that I'd like to thank. God, from whom all my blessings flow, my parents, grandparents, my great-grandfather, my late great-grandmother, and family, Mr. Jon Allen, my best friends, Darius and Angelica, my office staff, assistants and hospital personnel, fellow colleagues and all of my "Tabithas.""

The audience applauded wildly. Dr. Morris hugged her. When they parted, she returned his stare with a passion she hadn't felt in years.

Chapter TWO

Toni's office was a definite representation of her life. Most impressive was the wall comprised of the art pieces created by her patients. In the opposite corner, sat two oversized leather chairs, and a glass end table in front of them adorned with coffee table books. Two beanbags were in the center of the room with a toy table atop a tic-tac-toe square carpet. Various crystal vases and bowls can be found throughout the room. The newest addition, last night's trophy, was placed on the glass credenza at the window between her desk and the conference table. The dominating color throughout the room, carpet, furniture and frame-mats was purple. In the two leather chairs was where she writes.

Toni reviewed the mail and stamped it accordingly for Jackie her assistant to handle. She sipped some tea and reviewed the day's charts. She had a pretty easy day ahead. Jackie had even scheduled time for a decent lunch, something that didn't happen often. Her usual schedule included 30 to 40 minutes for lunch, which was consumed at her desk. She called Daphne in, her physician's assistant, to review the charts and to make all necessary notes.

"Good morning, Dr. T. Your gown was beautiful last night. Carolyn called this morning to say they would courier over the plaque to hang in your office. What's on the docket for today?" Daphne was always upbeat and positive. She hoped to be a doctor someday, too.

"Thanks, Daphne. I did have a good time. I haven't relaxed like that in a while. I must find somewhere to go where I can dance. I miss that. It was one of those things that got pushed way down on the priority list during medical school.

"The docket for today is easy. Kiki did an excellent job of scheduling. However, I'll probably pay for it next week," she let out a light chuckle. "I'm glad Monday is a staff day. By the way, it's Kiki's turn to plan. I reviewed today's charts and made notes. The Armstrong twins are coming. Have you reviewed these?"

"No, not really."

"Well, look over my notes and let me know if you have any questions. The first appointment is at 9:30 a.m. I'll check with Kiki about Monday's schedule for rounds so we can decide what time you'll come in," Toni said.

"The rounds schedule is also on your desk. You discharged everyone except Danielle and Tim. So rounds will be short. They should both be able to go home no later than Monday. I can come in for the first appointment. Here comes Kiki," Daphne said, as she moved the chair so that Kiki could sit down.

"Good morning, Dr. T. So you like your schedule today?"

"Yes, but I just told Daphne that I'll probably have to pay for this next week." Toni laughed with Kiki.

"I thought you would," Kiki said, showing off her beautiful smile. She was always on some diet because, according to her, she has a weight problem. She weighed 115 pounds.

"Thank you, Kiki. Daphne, please check to see if our 9:30 appointment is here. Kiki, is Monday's staff meeting menu set up? I completed the schedule on Wednesday. Let's have the usual set-up, please. Kiki, really which day am I paying for this schedule?" Toni asked jokingly.

"Well, next week is primarily semi-annual or annual check-ups, so naturally I scheduled more. It should flow smoothly. I don't anticipate any snags. I left room for any emergencies that may arise, but I actually expect a smooth week. You know school starts in three weeks, so the check-ups will be scheduled like this until then. I thought about suggesting we reschedule staff meetings in the evening or on weekends so we can comfortably accommodate our clients."

"Okay, if you have a plan then we will go with it. I just know I usually pay for such treats. I just wanted a warning," Toni smiled.

Kiki continued, "Not this time. Yes, the menu is done. The caterer will be here at

11:45 a.m. as usual. I selected pasta chicken salad with tortilla soup. For dessert, we're having cheesecake miniatures. Jackie will be in to show you the full schedule after your first appointment. Jennifer is buzzing you. Daphne must be ready," Kiki said.

Toni went to room number two where Denise was having her first check-up with Toni. Her family had just moved to Houston from Dallas. The last time Toni had seen Denise's mother, Debra, she was about four months pregnant. Now Denise was fifteen months old and walking. She touched everything at her level. She reached up to Toni and immediately started babbling. Toni scooped her from the floor. She touched Toni's hair and earrings, then she removed her glasses and gave them to Daphne, who happened to be standing the closest. She finally settled on Toni's stethoscope and placed it around her own neck, and turned to show Debra. Debra blushed.

Toni smiled because of Denise's accomplishment. Toni placed her on the table and let Denise hear her own heartbeat. Denise listened and smiled and giggled.

"Can I listen?" Toni asked.

Denise nodded yes in response and sat perfectly still so Toni could hear her heart. She seemed excited to be visiting the office, and was very cooperative the entire time.

"Well, welcome back to Houston. Thank you for coming to see me."

"Toni, you know that I wouldn't have anyone else." Debra replied.

"It's good to see you. We'll have to do lunch soon."

Denise liked Toni's office the most. She ran toward the beanbag and, when it appeared she would not be stopping, Daphne winced. Daphne placed her hand on her heart as the 15-month-old-child stopped just before hitting the back of the chairs that faced Toni's desk.

"Bye, bye, Denise." Toni left Debra and Denise to visit the twins. Denise waved good-bye when Toni closed the door.

Toni knew she had one more patient after the twins, then lunch. She was excited. She planned to walk down the block to Dillard's and pick up some new shoes and a bottle of Pleasure cologne.

Morgan and Melanie were fun and they talked throughout the entire visit. They will be 5 soon and kindergarten—bound. They weren't dressed alike, though. They seemed more excited than usual, but they did well throughout the check-up.

Jason was her next patient. "I'm seven. I start second grade this year."

Toni had never known him to be shy, "Really?"

"I'm really mature, too."

She couldn't help but chuckle when he said it. She stopped to see the facial expression that accompanied his comment. Toni looked first at Jason, then turned slowly to examine his father's, Robert, face.

"Don't look at me. His little girlfriend taught him that." Robert seemed concerned.

Toni couldn't figure out why. Jason was only a child. She walked Jason out and returned to her office when her intercom buzzed.

Kiki spoke suspiciously, "You have a delivery."

Toni wondered why Kiki or Jackie didn't just bring it in to her. "Kiki, are you unable to bring it to me? If so, please have Jen, Jackie or Daphne bring it in. I'm on my way out. I have to run..."

Just as she attempted to finish her sentence, her door opened slowly and out from behind it stood Dr. Morris. She rose slowly from her chair in an effort to greet him, although it was a feeble attempt. She extended her hand, and he accepted it and brought it up to his lips. He then extended his other arm to offer her two-dozen purple roses in a huge crystal vase. Neither of them spoke.

Jackie finally broke the silence. "Excuse me, Doctors. Dr. T., please don't be upset. I was sure you wouldn't mind since these are your absolute favorites." She smiled shyly and disappeared.

Finally, Dr. Morris spoke to a speechless Toni. "Dr. T.? Is that what they call you? How affectionate. I'm sure you are wondering why I'm here. Well that's easy, I'm here to escort you to lunch. No excuses allowed. I did it right too, I cleared it with your whole staff. So shall we?"

Hesitantly, she accepted his hand. She grabbed her purse from her drawer. "Jackie, would you please go to Dillard's. I put some shoes on hold and I needed a new bottle of Pleasure cologne."

"Sure, Dr. T." Jackie replied. Toni waved to her staff. Kiki signaled the next appointment time, and as Toni let the door fall softly, she heard an eruption of giggles. She made a mental note to question them upon her return.

As she was seated at the elegant bistro, the maitre d' placed a napkin in her lap. The wine steward placed a wine menu in front of Dr. Morris while she received the listing of entrée selections.

"Forgive me for not talking. I'm really surprised and it's rare for me to be surprised.

And now, I'm astonished. To what do I owe this pleasure?" Toni inquired.

Dr. Morris responded slowly. "I spoke to our colleagues at length about you so I would be able to introduce you to an audience that could understand you. I also spoke to your staff earlier this week about you, your mannerisms and your practice. They each lit up when they spoke. So, I made arrangements for this to happen today. In short, I want to know for myself."

"Is there more on your intentions list? You realize that I'm dating someone. Or is this purely professional?" she responded as she sipped her water.

"I do realize that you are seeing someone and I hope that you are not offended by this gesture. I wanted to talk to you. You inspired me last night. I wanted to talk to you more than ever. It is rare to meet someone who has it together and has a positive presence. Forgive me for being so forward. It meant a lot for me to give you that award. The smile on your face; that single tear. You are truly inspiring. I'd better stop babbling before you never want to talk to me again." Philip stopped talking just as lunch arrived.

They ate in silence for a few minutes before Toni asked Philip about his career, his personal life among other things. He told her he had been in private practice for about six years. He was 36 years old, never married and no children. He was from Lufkin, Texas and was a neurosurgeon. He attended at the same hospital system as Toni, although they had not seen each other often. He was the oldest of two siblings, one sister. He had recently bought a townhouse in very quiet neighborhood next to the hospital.

"I am currently looking for some property near the same area. I plan to build a home in the next three to four months. I have had very little time to property hunt, though. I was planning to look later next week," Toni said.

"Call me if you need help. But somehow I know you have it under control." He smiled.

"Thank you for the dance. I haven't felt like that in years." Toni paused and reflected on the gala.

"Toni, I wish I could say that I'm not interested but I am. I like everything about you. I was so excited to introduce you last night. I had a hard time turning you a loose after the dance."

"I was just telling my staff that I missed that." She responded purposely avoiding his comments.

"I know. Me, too." Philip noting her avoidance.

At the front of her building, he opened her door, reached for her hand, and she entered his embrace. When they finally released, she could only wave bye. Her efforts to speak failed her. He returned her wave with a smile.

She closed her office door and leaned on it. Her exhale was interrupted by the phone.

"Toni, where have you been? Jackie said you went to lunch. What took you so long?" Jon seemed irritated.

"Jon, what is the problem? I went to lunch. I ate. What's the big deal? Please calm down. Look, I've got to go. I've got patients to see. I'll be ready at 6:30 tomorrow. Talk to you later."

"I'm sorry, Toni. I'll see you tomorrow. Remember dressy casual. I'll be there at 6:30."

Jon hung up rather reluctantly, hoping she would talk a little longer. He often felt she was slipping away. He didn't know what the next move should be. He was afraid to ask her what to do. He knew he loved Toni, but didn't know how much. He didn't know if she was *in* love with him and he didn't want to find out. He did know that once she knew his fears, his chances for progression would be slim. Forever was a long time. Sometimes he feared her success. She had a comfort zone and confidence level all her own. He knew, most importantly, that he was limited on time. She was a wonderful woman, a definite asset to anything she touched. She was strong, focused, determined and full of spirit. She rarely wavered and rarely changed her mind. She had changed very little in eleven years. She was also a very planned person. He needed a plan to keep her, and quick.

At the time they met, Jon was attending a networking luncheon for Merrill Lynch as an intern. He would return to American University in D.C. where he would graduate in May.

Toni interned at Texas Commerce Bank with a corporate attorney and attended University of Houston to prepare for the fall semester. Her original intention was to become an attorney.

She disappeared. Before he could catch his breath, she was standing behind him asking if he enjoyed the view. His cinnamon complexion turned beet-red. He turned to her as she giggled and introduced herself as Antoinette M. Harden. He returned her handshake and said his name was Jonathon Allen. They talked for about twenty minutes before exchanging phone numbers. She said she had to go and he wished her a good day.

Toni reflected on lunch and relished the atmosphere. She realized that she missed the intimacy she felt at lunch. "Enough about that," she thought. She must get it together to move ahead with the rest of her plans for the year.

Chapter Three

She and Jon were going on their first date in three weeks on Saturday. Their last date was to a movie he selected and then promptly fell asleep after the first twenty minutes. When they left the theater, Toni had persuaded him to take her home saying she didn't feel well. Once she was home, she was furious. She waited until he called from his home then she left. She grabbed something to eat and returned to the movies to see the movie she originally wanted to see. When she finally returned home, she fell into bed from exhaustion. She decided she would simply avoid Jon's advances for future outings. This also meant that she had to avoid suggestions that they go anywhere. Since then, she treated herself to several movies, dinners, cultural outings and anything else she wanted. But for whatever reason, she was looking forward to going out with him on Saturday.

She accented her orange twin set, cream linen pants and orange sandals, with an orange clip in her hair, and gold jewelry. As she returned from the balcony, Jon rang the bell.

"You look gorgeous."

"Thank you. You look good yourself."

It was an intimate birthday gathering given for one of his fraternity brothers, Doug.

"Toni, this is Deirdre." Toni extended her hand to shake Dierdre's.

"Deirdre, it's nice to finally meet you. Doug always talks about you. I feel like I know you already."

Deirdre chuckled, "Same here, Toni. How's the property hunt?"

"Doug has been great. I'll be making a decision soon. Will I be hearing wedding bells soon?"

"We set the date for April. By the way, Doug and I would like for you to sing at our wedding."

"Sure, I will. I would be honored. Jon is actually excited about it. You know he says Doug got lucky."

"That is funny. Well, we'll keep in touch."

The evening was surprising, which included an evening stroll. The conversation was light, but good. They hadn't talked like that in a while. She knew Jon was scared of where she was headed, but she didn't know how to put him at ease. She wasn't sure she wanted to put him at ease. She just needed to keep with her life plan and not get caught up in his drama. The drive home was relaxed. He walked her to the door and kissed her goodnight.

"I'll pick you up at seven for church." Toni offered. They often went to church together. She thought it would bring them closer if they shared religion. It helped…somewhat.

She arrived at Jon's apartment within twenty minutes. She was surprised he wasn't ready yet. He was usually ready when she arrived. She had never noticed some of his knickknacks. She noticed a figurine of a little girl wearing a blue dress and braids. She was really cute. Toni wondered if there was a story behind the piece. She looked through his CD collection to see if he had any new discs. He usually bought rap and jazz music. She usually bought R&B and jazz, but they rarely had the same discs. He was finally ready after 15 minutes of her roaming.

Sunday morning was so beautiful. The sunlight was stunning. The birds were chirping. Toni felt great. The church was in a wooded area in an elite part of town. Darius, Toni's best friend, designed it. The outside had a cathedral effect, and the inside was more contemporary. Darius said that he imagined a room that would be comfortable to be in and just as beautiful. When he first presented the design and made the model, the building committee members were all so overwhelmed and excited, they voted approval immediately. The 2,600 seat church including the educational annex and additional parking, was built within fourteen months. The more intimate chapel-type sanctuary seats about 250. Toni recalled how the congregation grew when they built the building.

Pastor Allen was known for his instructional and proactive sermons. The congregation consisted of a mostly young population, predominately single, professional and financially stable. Pastor Allen was sensitive to the differences in the spirituality and practices, and tailored the format of his sermon, and the operation of the church, with the membership's youth in mind. It was definitely not Toni's grandparents' idea of a traditional Baptist church.

Pastor Allen made a strong statement when he encouraged the trustees to elect some women to the board. He recommended Toni and another woman, who was an attorney. He let the board know that these times called for change, and change needed to happen across the gender lines. He recommended them because of their contributions to the community. When the board approved them, Toni was truly surprised. Her commitment to the board was unwavering. The ten-member board of trustees revolutionized the Baptist Church Conference by electing women.

After the service, Toni waved to Darius and Angelica as they approached the door to exit the church. Toni stepped to the side so she could visit with them while Jon headed to the car. Angelica hugged Toni in congratulations. They hadn't talked since the awards ceremony. Darius snuck in a kiss to Toni's cheek when Angelica let her go.

Darius gained so much credibility after the church's completion that he became a partner in the architecture firm where he worked. Previously, he had contemplated leaving the firm to start his own office. His boss must have sensed it because after the church appeared in *Architecture Digest*, he immediately promoted Darius to partner. Darius believed it had a lot to do with the fact that when he took the job to his boss, he turned Darius down cold. Darius took it as an extra job, as he did with similar projects, especially those that involved friends or causes about which he felt strongly. He earned quite a bit of respect doing outside projects, which was enough motivation to start his own firm. He decided to take the position as partner because he had more creative license as a partner, and he could inherit the firm when his boss retires. His boss had no family and no son to succeed him in the business. Since Darius had become a partner, the firm's profits had nearly doubled.

Darius and Toni had been best friends for several years. They had met at Howard

University. Darius thought the world of Toni, and he protected her like a sister at school. He was three years older and a junior when she arrived at school. They became closer after his father died. He completed the semester with a decent grade point average thanks to Toni. She mailed his assignments, faxed them to his sister, sent them home with his friends and called him on the phone.

When he was selected to give the graduation address, his powerful speech moved the crowd to their feet with a thunderous eruption of applause. He told the entire audience that his inspiration to succeed and finish school was now shared between his father and his best friend. He told the story of his senior year when "his little sister" got him through school. He dedicated his diploma to his father and his best friend, Toni. He closed the speech with a poem from Nikki Giovanni, "Ego Tripping," Toni's favorite. Darius promised to be there for her, and he always had.

He was excited to be designing her home. "Don't forget about lunch this week. The plans are almost ready." They hadn't done lunch in a while. They were both looking forward to it.

Angelica reminded, "Call me." Angelica always had gossip.

Just then Jon pulled up and got out of the car. He came up and spoke to Darius and Angelica, but Jon was never talkative when they were around.

Jon and Toni decided to go to The Redwood Grill for lunch. After they ordered, they discussed her investment portfolio. He was a stockbroker and her personal investment advisor. He had been with A.G. Edwards for about six years, and he was trying to establish enough clientele to start his own firm. His goal was to start the company in March of next year, so he had about six more months to put plans in place and execute them. Knowing him though, Toni figured he probably wouldn't. His indecisiveness frustrated her.

Jon changed the subject. "Toni, you looked really gorgeous at the ball. I was the envy of every man in the room. Your work inspires me. When I hear about your work like that, I get renewed. But it shouldn't take that. I feel like I'm missing parts of your life."

Toni sighed and nodded in agreement. She knew in her heart that Jon did not really want children. She decided against commenting on the remark he made about missing parts of her life. She also knew that she wanted at least one child. She had come from a single-parent home with one older brother. Her family was small and she wanted more than what she had in her family. Family was important to her. Their priorities were different.

She had seriously considered adoption because so many babies need homes. But he was adamant that he did not want any children in his life that were not his. She felt he was being selfish. He didn't really understand her commitment to the children. They never formally agreed to disagree but they never reached a resolve, either.

"Let's change the subject please," Toni suggested. She always became withdrawn when he was being selfish and more importantly that their views on children differed in such major ways. Their relationship grew distant proportionately to their differences about children.

He could sense her frustration, "We need to discuss our upcoming trip for your birthday."

He always wanted to take her somewhere for her birthday, but Toni was so focused on her work and goals that last year she canceled a week before they were to leave. This time, he had planned it down to the final detail and made sure she cleared her schedule and just to pack for warm weather.

"I'm glad you are letting me surprise you. I'm so excited. Are you looking forward to it?" Jon questioned.

Her response was flat, "Yes, I am."

He was excited, but she wasn't and didn't know why. She wasn't looking forward to her birthday.

Chapter Four

Toni drove to the small suburban area near the church where the properties were located. She selected the larger lot. It had been hard to decide because she liked the corner lot, yet she thought the lot at the end of the street would also be nice. It was positioned in a cul-de-sac and was trapezoid-shaped. In addition, there was a 25,000-square-foot lake behind the lot with geese, fish and swans. She had already envisioned reading in the bay window overlooking the beautiful water. There was a pier at the base of the lake at each home.

She always wanted this house—the perfect one. One where she could retreat from the whole world and do her favorite things: write and read while listening to music. She always wanted to select a home with her husband but she didn't know how long that would take. So she decided to go for her dream house alone.

"Do you want to go to the Galleria?"

"That's fine," Jon agreed.

As they approached the ice skating rink, Jon asked, "It's been a long time since we skated. Want to?"

"Sure. Why not?" Toni reflected on how the relationship had been in the beginning. Skating reminded her of the fun they once had. They had spent hours together talking, shopping and doing whatever they wished. They were so fulfilled, so happy. Then one day things were different. One day she felt different. She felt she was all alone. She felt she had outgrown Jon.

Of course, his drinking affected her also. Their last argument didn't go well. She remembered the incident like it was yesterday. She thought she had fallen asleep before he called but actually he never called. The next morning he called and asked her to come pick him up. Toni agreed without question. When she arrived, her shock overwhelmed her. He had been drinking with his friends. According to him, he thought he only had a couple of drinks. She later found out that he had several Kamukazi's. He didn't remember anything. Particularly how his truck sat on four flat tires.

When she arrived at his house, he hung his head as the wrecker towed his truck to the nearest tire store for replacements. She considered asking but she could never make her words audible. He promised then to stop drinking but never quite kept that promise. Nothing he could muster as an excuse could make her tears stop falling.

When she finally approached the subject again, "You don't seem to understand that I don't want to be close to you if you don't intend to take of care of yourself or put yourself in danger on a regular basis. This is not normal behavior."

"I know," he held his head down.

"You can't possibly know. You use drinking to run from your problems; which ones I don't know. When I ask you what's wrong or what's going on, you say nothing. Or you just act like I didn't say anything." She yelled.

"I can't make you understand. I think you will judge me." He yelled.

"The bigger issue is that you have put your life in danger several times. You cannot be responsible for other lives if this is how you care for your own. Your behavior is inexcusable. Your reaction and lack of responsibility make me bitter towards you." Toni pouted.

"Well what do you want me to do? You just don't understand."

"But when I try, you shut me out or you avoid the issue. What am I supposed to do with that?"

He stormed out. She cried in anger. She vowed to let the relationship go. The next day he apologized, sent flowers, met her at the hair salon, and took her to lunch. He assumed all was forgiven and forgotten. He assumed wrong. She was still incredibly bitter.

They called each other when it was convenient. They still liked each other. She just wished he was the one and he's not. At least not now. Today was no different. She used the cautious approach.

"I thought you stopped drinking?" She referred to the glass at the ball. She looked over her shoulder for a response.

He shook his head in disbelief, "So you believe I was drinking on Thursday?"

"Yes, I believe I smelled the liquor on your breath. So, I'll just ask. Were you drinking alcohol mixed with coke on Thursday?"

"Yes, I was drinking a bourbon and soda. What's the big deal?"

She responded slowly. "I thought you decided it was best not to drink in public. I was just hoping you had gotten past the point where it seemed you needed to drink at every occasion. At any rate, you promised. When you break a promise, usually an explanation is due and an apology expected. I was just hoping you realized how it affects me."

"Toni, I apologize; that's all I can say. I really apologize. I'm working through the drinking issue. It's hard sometimes. I've even thought of getting professional help. I just don't have the courage to go." He lowered his head and then looked out the window. He put his hands together on the table and looked down at them.

She looked into his eyes and assured him that she was on his side. "I told you I will go to the meetings or counseling or whatever with you. Just let me know." She wanted to help but this was the last one of these conversations she intended to endure. The tension that resulted was too much for her to bear.

She decided to drive around after she drove Jon home, "I'll go to the old neighborhood first," she thought aloud. "I haven't been there since high school."

Her mother had remarried and sold the house. After college, she was on her own. She bought the townhouse before she left Johns Hopkins. After graduation from medical school, she was worried about moving back to Houston since she had been gone for so long. Toni's mom didn't really extend her support. Her brother was too self-absorbed. He was probably separated by that time. Her family became the hospital staff, colleagues, other residents and interns, and of course, Darius and Angelica.

Darius came to her rescue. He invited her to the church she now attends. She was complete, but could use some additional avenues.

She transferred her membership with her sorority, which had its perks. It had the fellowship she was lacking and it had connections, which were essential. After her activity with the sorority resumed, she was inducted into the Links, Inc., a prestigious group of women who put networking on a whole new plane. One of her college mentors sponsored her membership. With these activities, she no longer needed the family security for which she had prayed. She did things with them but was not dependent on them. She did want to maintain a special relationship with her niece, who needed support on many issues in her life.

After she left the old neighborhood, she decided to drive by her old high school. She hadn't seen it since graduation. Now it was fully renovated and looked like a college campus, which made her proud. She remembered the reunion would be approaching soon. She would never forget kissing Damon on the steps near her chemistry class. Nor would she forget catching Jesse kissing another girl. She wouldn't forget her senior English teacher. She couldn't possibly forget the teacher that died. It was so sad and sobering. Of course, she couldn't forget her play brother who took care of her and vice versa. "Where was he now," she wondered. She would never forget the shopping center around the corner was so small and now it makes her forget what it used to look like. It has become a major center with several anchor stores. They replaced the sandwich shop with some salad place. "Those were the good old days," she thought.

One the drive home, she stopped at the bookstore. She selected four books, including *Love Poems*, by Nikki Giovanni, her favorite poet. She was paying the bill when her pager beeped. She got in the car and called her answering service immediately. The service stated that John Harper was being rushed to Texas Children's Hospital emergency room. As she drove, she paged Daphne.

"Dr. T, I'm on my way," Daphne rushed.

"Okay, Daphne. Be careful. See you there." Toni closed her phone.

When Toni got to the hospital, John was just arriving. She got all the vitals from the EMS team. She and the chief of trauma started work immediately. The symptoms led Toni to believe John was having an asthma attack.

After minutes, John's attack subsided. He was breathing close to normal and he had opened his eyes, both of which were good signs. They moved him to a temporary patient room. Toni prescribed some medicine and they promised to monitor him. She made an appointment for him on Monday. Just as she was leaving, Dr. Morris walked in to the ER. He moved so swiftly, he nearly knocked Toni down.

"I'm sorry, Toni. I didn't mean to run you over. My nephew was just rushed in. I'm looking for him." Philip looked past Toni to find his family.

"What's your nephew's name?"

"John. John Harper. There's my sister." He attempted to move around Toni.

"John is my patient. He is recovering. He had an asthma attack." She took his hand and walked him to the doctor's lounge and attempted to calm him down.

Philip then confided in Toni, "My sister doesn't make the best decisions. Her husband manipulates her. I don't like that. I've tried to help with medical issues, but was rejected. I considered not coming, but I realize that my nephew shouldn't suffer just because we don't agree on everything. I love John and I want the best for him." Philip exhaled.

"Do you want me to stay while you visit John?" Toni's hand was still in his.

"No, you were headed home. I'm sure you're tired. I'll call you if I have any questions." He walked her to the ER doors and went back to see John.

Of her three messages, she called Angelica back first. She knew it was gossip so she wanted it over with as soon as possible.

"Hey Jelly, how are you? You looked great at church today."

"Toni, thanks. I noticed Jon was distant today. Is there anything wrong?" she slowly questioned. Toni was fairly private, and Angelica knew to wait for her rather than ask knowing that she and Jon were a sensitive issue right now.

"Jon is being very distant and I'm letting him. He is being overly sensitive. He has shut me out before and I just ride the storm, he'll be fine. How's the new beau in your life? I know that there is one."

"I don't really have one. I had to let that last guy go because he was stalker material. He wanted to call all the time. I canceled a date with him and he flipped completely out. Girl, I had to read him on the spot. I can't tolerate that ignorance. Anyway, the real reason I called was to tell you that I got a promotion. I'm now the Vice President of

Community Affairs and Government Relations. I was so excited I could hardly hold it. I told Darius on Thursday. I got busy on Friday and couldn't call you."

"Jelly, congratulations. You really deserve it. You have been with the bank awhile and you've always liked your job. Do you have to move at all?"

"I have to move downtown where I'll have a staff and be the leader of the team that insures that we are involved in the community especially those where we have branches. We coordinate our efforts with marketing and public relations. It is, of course, all based on image. Well, I'd better go. I go to the new office tomorrow. I'll call Jackie with the new numbers."

"Congratulations, again. Now that you're closer, maybe we can do lunch sometime. Talk to you later." She hung up with Angelica wondering what transformations were taking place in her life. This position will expose her artistry. She'll be really happy to be doing something that involves the community.

As she prepared to call Jon, she arranged her books on the bookshelf. She placed one of the newest selections on the nightstand. She hit the speed dial button for Jon but only got his machine. "Jon, this is Toni. Call me when you get this message."

By the time Darius said hello, she was sunken into the Italian leather chaise lounge.

"What's going on?"

"Nothing much. I just relaxed after church."

"I decided on the cul-de-sac." Toni leaned back with her book cradled in her lap. "I really love it. I don't know why it took me so long to decide."

Darius moved away from his light table to the sofa, "I designed something perfect for that spot. I somehow knew that you would pick that lot."

"Hey, can we change tomorrow to dinner? I have our staff meeting."

"Cool. La Griglia's okay?"

"Yeah. We haven't been there in awhile."

"I'll pick you up at 5:30. Did you speak to Jelly?"

"Yes, I have."

"She told you about the promotion, huh?"

"Yes. I'm real proud of my sister-friend."

"Anyway, as for the house, I used the specifications that you gave me on the design. I also added some things that I thought would suit your style. So, let's review the plans at dinner."

"Let me know who the builders are. I have someone out of town that I know that I want to have the opportunity to place a bid. At any rate, I'm so ecstatic about my plans." Toni sighed as she leaned back in the chaise.

"What's going on between you and Jon? He doesn't have a clue does he? I sometimes wonder when he lost it." Darius chuckled.

"I'm still seeing him. He's at a loss right now. I'm not sure where he's going with this. I don't want to marry him though. I know that. Well anyway, I need to get to bed. I'll page you when I'm through with rounds." She hung up the phone and went upstairs. Just as she reached the top of the stairs, the phone rang.

"Hey, you." Jon tried to sound upbeat.

"Hi, Jon. What's going on? You sounded dry on your message." She readied herself for bed.

"I was on the phone with Mother when you called. She's coming next weekend. She made these arrangements without asking me." Jon heaved a heavy sigh.

"Well, did she say why she was coming?" Toni wondered what could be wrong with her that she was coming back so soon. She was just here a few weeks ago and doesn't like to travel.

"She didn't say. On top of which, her plane lands at 10 on Saturday. I have a seminar that morning."

"I'll pick her up. She'll want to shop anyway. How long did she say she would be staying?"

"She didn't say. Probably her usual here on Saturday, gone on Sunday." Jon fiddled with the phone cord, "Thank you, Toni for your help. You two sure do get along better than we seem to."

Toni climbed into bed, "As a matter of fact, she can stay with me if she wants. You know I don't mind."

"Well again, thanks. What'd you do after you dropped me off?" Jon moved to his bedroom window, overlooking the pool in his complex.

"The bookstore. An emergency at the hospital. The music store. Talked to Jelly, who got promoted last week. All in a Sunday afternoon." She let out a lighthearted chuckle.

"I've been thinking a lot about us lately. I love you. And I care for you. I realize that we aren't as close as we used to be." Jon leaned against the windowsill.

Toni moved nervously in her bed. "Your mother asked you why you hadn't asked me to marry you, huh?"

"Yeah." Jon lowered his head.

"I'm not in a rush." Toni closed her eyes hoping this conversation would end soon. "Marriage is a lifestyle, which requires a change. That's not what I want right now. I'm not in a hurry."

"You in the bed?"

"Yeah."

"I'll talk to you tomorrow." Jon pushed the off button on his cordless wondering if that conversation could've gone any worse.

He spoke aloud, "Did she say that she didn't want to marry me or that she's not in a hurry to marry me?"

He slammed his fist against the wall in frustration. He hoped that their upcoming vacation would rekindle the love they once had.

He thought she wanted to be married. To him. Now, he didn't really know what her goals were. Her building a home intimidated him. He was fully aware that she could live without him. Toni's beauty, inner and outer, didn't help. She turned heads with her toned body and Bailey's and cream skin and her long, golden brown hair. He couldn't afford to lose by most standards the perfect mate.

Often Jon felt that she didn't need him to validate her being nor to quantify her success. As he dressed, he considered what he should do next.

He went running to mull over his thoughts. He could no longer afford to neglect her feelings. He couldn't keep quiet. He ran faster when he realized that he had stopped doing what attracted her in the beginning. He shouted in the dark, "I'm stupid!"

He ran faster. He had to make this vacation count. Pull out all the stops!

Chapter Five

"Table for two, non-smoking please," Darius said, confidently. His 6'2" frame towered confidently over her 5'7" frame. She studied his face as they waited for a table. His smooth, cinnamon complexion, hazel-green eyes, and well-defined cheekbones, generally caused women in his proximity to drool. While they admired his baby-fine hair, they usually envied Toni when she stood at his side.

His style only added to their lustful glances. Today his Armani houndstooth suit and crisp white custom tailored tab collar shirt with French cuffs, accentuated his athletic physique. His brown Brooks Brothers shoes matched his silk chocolate Hugo Boss tie. A hint of Ferragamo followed him.

The hostess tried not to melt at the sound of his sexy voice. "Sure, follow me," she stammered.

Darius ordered a bottle of Riesling. As the wine arrived, Darius unrolled the plans, which were quite detailed. Toni carefully examined each corner of her home. Darius reviewed the process with her.

"Copyrighting takes about a week. I'll add the things we've mentioned, then submit the original for copyrights. After you've made your selections, then we'll start building. I'm so excited for you. By the way, your lender called today wanting an estimate so they can complete your loan documents. I'm sure she'll be calling you tomorrow."

Toni's plans showed a five-bedroom house with five and one-half baths, and entertainment rooms. In addition, it featured a formal living and dining area, a den and an office. The gourmet-style kitchen was designed to include a double island with a half cutting area and half grill, and a hanging pot rack. The house would have a two-car garage, built-in bookshelves, built-in benches under the bay windows, vaulted ceilings and sunken floors in the formal areas. The deck would include a pool and hot tub. Toni's favorite amenity was the three built-in aquariums. Darius knew she was satisfied.

"Toni, I love you because you inspire me. I have been looking for property and working on some designs for a while, but was never encouraged to build on my own until you decided to do it. I remember what you said about not waiting and I've waited long enough. I've been searching for a staff of homebuilders. I'm looking to partnership with, or to hire a homebuilder and start a company separate from, yet affiliated with, the firm. We would buy land for subdivisions and build homes to sell. I've even talked to some investors. This is a big step for me, Toni. I stand to gain quite a bit of money, as will the firm. When I first mentioned the idea to Mr. Patterson, he was apprehensive but he came around. He thinks I'll do it with or without him. What do you think?"

"Darius, that sounds wonderful. It's a big step but what isn't? I'd like to consider investing. Email me the info, or send it with the page layouts of the house. Also, you may want to share your ideas with Jon so he can help with investors. Where do you want the project?"

"My first choice is the Heights. My second choice would be Third Ward. They both have some undeveloped land, as well as some underdeveloped land. The building company will be able to bid to refurbish homes to sell. This will be specifically targeted at Housing and Urban Development, VA or Federal Housing Administration foreclosures."

"Do you have a real estate agent?"

"No, we don't have an agent or an attorney. I'd appreciate your recommendations both of these positions. I do appreciate the fact that you're thinking about investing. Thanks."

"By the way, an attorney can act as a real estate agent once you decide what you want to buy. You can call and ask for list prices in your two chosen areas of interest. Then the attorney can prepare contracts you need and handle the set up of your new entity. One of my friends, my attorney's partner, can help in that respect. He has some real estate experience. Doug is my agent, if you want to use him." She placed her glass on the table nearly empty.

"Sounds good. I'll make those calls tomorrow. Thanks." He placed his napkin on the table and poured Toni another glass of wine. "To change the subject, Toni, what are you doing this weekend?" Darius asked, as he finished his steak.

"I'll be spending the weekend with Jon's mother. We'll probably shop all weekend, go to church, eat lunch with Jon and then we'll put her back on the plane. She is a really sweet woman, but she's on Jon's back to do something more with his life. She wishes that we would get married. He's not ready, mentally or emotionally. We had a talk last night. I told him I was in no rush to get married. He seemed relieved. I knew this before our conversation. It is clear that he's not ready," Toni said.

"Have you considered leaving him? He doesn't seem to make you happy," Darius said.

"Well, right now he's a good party date. If he would improve his attitude and motivation, the relationship could probably move forward. We've been dating for nearly the eleven years I've known him and have made no real concrete decisions. I have goals that I need, and want to meet with, or without him. I've waited. Patiently, I might add. There is no real commitment. There is an understanding, but no pressure since I'm working on other things. Eventually I want to get married and have a child. I have stroked his ego for quite sometime. At this point, I'm worried about Toni's well-being."

"I see," Darius said, pondering over the situation.

He dropped Toni at her office to pick up her car. As he drove home, he wondered if Toni was under any emotional distress. She was considered a diva by sheer accomplishment. He knew she had been through the normal family drama, such as divorce, family fall-out, the arguments, and the family secrets. Her family has been far less than supportive. When she decided to become a doctor, she was determined to complete her undergraduate degree and then she got into the medical schools of her choice. All alone.

Medical school had been somewhat tough for her. While she was completing medical school, her great-grandmother became ill. Her great-grandmother was so very special to her. Toni praised her great-grandmother like she was a goddess. This great-grandmother was the one that shared with Toni the importance of such life matters as happiness, God, sharing, love and how to cook. Her great-grandmother spoiled her so. Toni lacked for nothing. When Toni's mother called, she was devastated. Toni didn't go to a mandatory practicum. She sunk so low to tell of her great-grandmother's death, that her finals had proved to be a real challenge. Her professors were very understanding, though. She still graduated valedictorian.

At the funeral, Toni sang a medley of her great-grandmother's favorite songs. Toni cried through the entire medley. Darius sat in the choir stand to support her. He had been worried. Prior to the funeral, she hadn't eaten in two days. In that span of six days, she managed to sleep only 12 hours. Her great-grandmother died on the second day of final exams. She decided to make the funeral arrangements. She had to debate with her grandmother and her father, but she made the arrangements anyway. She graduated in the morning, made the graduation speech and was on the plane in the afternoon. She completed the arrangements on Monday. She laid her grandmother to rest on Wednesday. In addition to Toni's solo, she and Jelly sang a duet.

Several of her relatives cried aloud at the church and some at the graveside. Toni was astounded. She had arranged for the graveside to be clear when they reopened the casket for her final private viewing. Darius didn't remember Jon being there. Jelly and Darius stood at the limo that waited to take Toni back to the house. Toni had sent her family ahead. Her great-grandfather had been extremely quiet and clung to Toni most of the services. He was proud to hear her sing. He hadn't heard her sing in several years. Darius noticed how close she was to her great-grandparents. He thought that was amazing. He didn't really know his great-grandparents or grandparents, for that matter. Toni deserved to have that experience. They were so very important to her.

Darius knew Jon wasn't always as supportive as he could be. He also knew that Toni needed an understanding man who was in tune to her well-being and emotional needs. Jon just wasn't that man. Darius had never really thought about this until dinner. He decided to talk to her about this again.

Toni finished her house budget and decided to read a book. She had just gotten comfortable when the phone rang. She decided against answering, and the machine picked up after the third ring. Just as she went back to her book, her pager beeped. She dialed Doug.

"Hello. You aren't answering the phone?" he asked.

"I was reading. I forgot I paged you. What's going on?" Toni held her page with a bookmark.

"Your property closed this afternoon." Doug placed her file in his credenza.

"I'm really sorry that I didn't meet the seller."

"Well, you finish your book. I'll talk to you tomorrow."

"By the way, Darius, my best friend, has designed the house. He has some revisions to make. By the end of the week, we'll be ready. I'm too excited. When the house is nearly complete, I want to list my condo for lease. You haven't been over since I made some changes. The carpet and appliances, including the washer and dryer are new. I'll make it available next week for a walk-through. Send over the necessary lease papers, too. Thanks again Doug."

"You're welcome, Toni. Goodnight."

Chapter six

She met Darius on the jogging track. He was stretching when she arrived. She stretched while teasing him about work.

"How can you exercise when you have so much work to do?" Toni laughed. She knew that Darius worked at home, too.

"You should be receiving a package tomorrow," Darius said. "When your copies are ready, they'll be delivered. You will be pleased; I sent them for copyrights today. We sent out the bid requests. They'll be back in two weeks as well." Toni picked up the pace slightly, as Darius glided in next to her. He was accustomed to her taking off without warning.

Toni thought she and Darius had run a shorter distance until she saw the counter display. They eased into the third mile in silence. The runs were always therapeutic because the solitude gave her time to think. She hadn't spoken to her mother in a while and thought about phoning her later. Her brother had left her a message the other day and she needed to return his call. She made mental notes of several projects to accomplish in the near future. She wanted to sponsor an etiquette seminar for preteens and teens at the clinic with her sorority sisters. She also wanted to mentor an aspiring pediatrician. Her mentor had taken her under his wing, and she decided to do the same.

She wondered what Darius had done on his newest project. He always impressed her. She glanced over to see Darius smirk.

"I thought about what you said the other day. I'm worried about your happiness. It doesn't seem like you have what you want," he said.

"I'm not having a problem with my happiness. God is responsible for that. Work and my community commitments keep me busy enough. Now my social life is a different story. In our eleven years, Jon has become less involved in my life and less socially active. My thoughts about our future have diminished significantly. I will be making more of an effort to enjoy myself whether he can participate or not. I see fun stuff in my future. I work hard. I deserve to play hard. I'm not holding my breath waiting for Jon to step up."

"So what about marriage? I thought you wanted that." Darius questioned.

"As for marriage, I have a vision of marriage that he doesn't understand. I don't subscribe to the idea that you marry on a time schedule because you're 27 or 31. If you get married because of age, or because the biological clock is ticking, your marriage is sure to fail. I want to marry a man who I'll enjoy waking up to for the rest of my life, because I love him, because we have some things in common, because I can share, travel, read and play with him. I could have children alone. Adoption would be my preference, or even artificial insemination. Without the proper preparation, the wedlock could be dissolved before the child is born. I want to have a child based on what I have to offer, rather than depending on what someone else has to offer. I can only depend on what I bring to the table because as we see, those things can change. Anyway, I have several more things to accomplish before I become responsible for someone else's life.

"Besides," Toni laughed, "I still need to get to the ski slopes. Do you think we can ski over Thanksgiving? We haven't been on a trip together in a while. Us and some friends. Are you game?" Toni quickened the pace again slightly.

"It has been a long time since we have been anywhere together. I guess I can find someone to take. There's an attorney I've been seeing. Maybe she can go. Are you going to have your travel agent to make the arrangements? Where do you want to go anyway?"

"What about Vail? You've been there?" She paused briefly.

"Yeah. I liked it, too. Last year's summit was there. Aspen might be a good choice, as well. Your travel agent should be able to get us some great deals. If not, let me know and my agent can do it. By the way, who are you going to take?" Darius chuckled, knowing she wouldn't appreciate the laughter.

"That's for me to know, and for you to find out," she said, laughing. They were nearing the end of their six-mile run. After they walked another half mile, she stretched while he jumped rope. She was trying to decide whether to cook or get a salad on the way home, when Darius interrupted her thoughts.

"Would you like to come over to eat?" he asked.

"I think I'll pass. I need to make some phone calls, and some notes for Jackie. I'll take a rain check though."

♦♦♦♦♦♦

After she made a list for Jackie, she completed the articles and began work on her résumé, the phone rang simultaneously with the doorbell. She grabbed the cordless phone on her way to the door. Jon's mother was on the phone, and Jon was at the door. She smiled and motioned to him to be quiet.

"Hello, Mrs. Allen. I hear that you're coming to visit." Toni locked the door behind Jon. She sat on the sofa opposite him.

Mrs. Allen had probably just spoken with Jon and he was, no doubt, here to vent his frustration with her. At any rate, his disappointed look was enough repayment for coming by without calling. She leaned back to get comfortable because she knew the conversation would be intense.

"Hello, Toni. Well I trust Jon spoke to you about my visit this Saturday," Mrs. Allen said.

"Yes, he did. I'm looking forward to seeing you again," Toni replied.

"He told me you're picking me up. I hope that's okay. I told him I didn't want to impose. I intended to spend the weekend with him and not bother you. You're really sweet to take time out for me," Mrs. Allen said, pausing for a moment. Toni wasn't sure if she had finished speaking.

"It was my idea. Really it's not any trouble at all. We'll go shopping and maybe even the ballet. I can get "Cinderella" tickets."

Mrs. Allen was thrilled with Toni's suggestions. "You always make me feel welcome. Those are wonderful ideas."

All the while, Toni had the feeling she wanted to discuss other matters of greater importance. "Mrs. Allen, you seem to have something on your mind. Do you want to talk about it?"

"Yes, I do. I didn't want to bother you with it, but I was hoping Jon would have asked you to marry him. I want so much for you two to become a couple. I don't know what he's doing. I think he's going to lose you if he continues to wait. I've said too much, haven't I? Don't tell him I said this to you. He would be upset that I shared these feelings with you. I guess I'd better go. I'll see you on Saturday at 10. I'll be at Hobby on Southwest. See you soon." Mrs. Allen fidgeted with the phone.

"Don't worry about this, Mrs. Allen. Things always work out for the best. Your secrets are safe with me. You need not be worried; I'll see you on Saturday. Be sure to call if anything changes." Toni replaced the phone on the charger.

The look on Jon's face was priceless. "Toni, I don't believe she called you. She has no business doing that. I just can't get away with anything without her assistance and meddling. I'm so sick of it. I wish she would let me live my life in my own way. My brother told me this would happen."

"Look, don't worry about it. She'll be here a couple of days and then she'll go back to San Antonio. You have to let this go. Why do you let this get to you? She just wants you to be happy. She wants another grandchild. You know that she loves you.

"Maybe if you had a more active social live, you'd have more to tell her. Then she'd think things were going well and leave you alone. You need to become more proactive in your life." Toni put her hand to her mouth in an effort to retrieve those hurtful words.

Jon shook his head in disbelief. He just couldn't get it together. Yet, he needed to, desperately. On the drive home, he thought about what Toni had said. He could become active in his fraternity again. He could actively seek new clients, and it was time to put that business plan on paper. He reasoned that his involvement in more activities would captivate Toni's attention again. He needed to start somewhere.

The weekend came, and Mrs. Allen was on time as usual. She always traveled light, and never checked baggage. Mrs. Allen generally shopped a great deal when she traveled, so there was no need for a lot of luggage. She hugged Toni tightly at the gate. She was wearing a bright sundress and matching sandals.

The first stop was lunch. They always ate at America's first. Toni and Jon had taken her there once, and she loved it. She called Jon from the car on the way to let him know she had arrived. The stairs in the restaurant made Toni nervous because Mrs. Allen was wearing her 'sexy' sandals that are never quite stable. Toni had only been able to persuade her to use the elevator once.

After lunch, they arrived at Neiman Marcus amidst the Saturday rush. Toni was trying on a pair of Ferragamo pumps when Mrs. Allen became serious.

After being quiet for the better portion of the day, Mrs. Allen broke her silence, "Toni, I'm sick. I've been preparing for my passing."

"The boys have always made sure I was taken care of, and now I want to make sure they are taken care of. I have made all the funeral arrangements."

Toni interrupted, "Mrs. Allen, please don't say that. That's awful. What would make you do that?"

Mrs. Allen ignored her comments, "Everything is paid for, and I have a folder marked in my file cabinet. In addition, the life insurance policies, the will and other property deeds are there as well. I paid off all my bills. I added Jon to all my accounts and to the property deeds so he wouldn't have any problems handling anything. I didn't do it when Jon's dad passed, but I had them transferred to me so all Jon has to do is follow my instructions and probate my will.

"I'm telling you all of this because I want you to be there for him when this happens. When I talk about death, he completely tunes me out. You have been the daughter that I've never had. Now sweetie, I don't want to dwell on this all day. If you have anything else to say, please say it now." She looked like a weight had been lifted off her shoulders. She seemed so relieved and relaxed; it was unbelievable.

Mrs. Allen's announcement rendered Toni speechless. Toni could barely see beyond the tears that welled in her eyes. Jon would be devastated. Toni reached out and hugged her. She whispered that she loved her, and promised to help Jon through.

Mrs. Allen took another deep breath, wiped tears from Toni's eyes and tried to continue browsing as if nothing were wrong. Toni reflected on life for a moment, and reaffirmed that it was too short to be unhappy. Not even for a moment.

Toni tried to hide her sadness. They shopped all the way from Neimans to Saks Fifth Avenue and back. The ballet led to an impromptu decision to buy elegant ball gowns. Their glitzy attire surprised Jon. The limo driver at the door was his second surprise.

The ballet made Jon realize he needed to love Toni the way she deserved. She shouldn't have had to plan that type of evening for them. That should have been his responsibility. Again, he had missed something significant.

Raymond, the executive vice-president the Houston Ballet, introduced her to each of the dancers. She was totally captivated. Toni and Jon watched silently as they moved around the Green Room. Toni and Lauren spoke briefly before Lauren disappeared to change so they could leave. Half an hour later, the six of them were eating dinner. Toni sat between Jon and Raymond. Raymond talked to Toni most of the evening. She sensed Jon's nervousness and jealously surfacing.

Mrs. Allen raved about the event during the entire meal. She couldn't wait to tell her best friend about meeting the lead dancer, an African American woman, Lauren Anderson.

On their way to the airport, Mrs. Allen spoke in a low tone. "Jon, I have breast cancer. I start chemotherapy when I get home."

Jon looked straight ahead. He mumbled, "How long have you known?" Toni heard the hurt in his voice.

"I've seen three doctors. I'm still in prayer about the outcome. God is still in charge. Don't you forget that." Mrs. Allen touched his hand.

He looked down at her hand. "Mom, I'm sorry. I'll be there next week," he whispered.

Toni stood on the perimeter to respect Jon and his mother's moment of privacy. In truth, she was trying to give Jon a chance to respond freely. On the ride home Jon spoke very little. He dropped Toni at home without walking her to the door.

Chapter seven

"May I have your attention please?" Darius asked, politely tapping his glass to get everyone's attention. "Thank you for joining us to warm Toni's house. Please raise your glass with me. Toni, your determination to do bigger and better things is simply inspiring. Cheers to my dear friend, and a toast to a wonderful woman who deserves the very best," Darius said, smiling.

"Thank you so much for coming. You need to know that my best friend, Darius, designed my home. Let's toast to Darius, a phenomenal man and architect. Please eat, drink and enjoy. I'll be giving a tour in a minute." She hugged Darius and Jelly.

After the final guest left, Toni kicked off her Italian sandals. Darius and Jelly helped her move gifts from the foyer to the entertainment room. They were relaxing when the doorbell rang.

Jelly returned with a huge floral arrangement in a crystal vase. As usual, Jelly was being nosey. She inspected the vase as she placed it on the table and instantly grabbed the card. Jelly handed the card to Toni and waited with baited breath. Toni blushed as she opened the card. Her smile spread as she read aloud, "I'm sorry that I wasn't able to make your gathering. I would like to make it up to you later this week. Sincerely, Raymond."

Jelly announced, "Competition is good for the soul." Jelly was glad Toni attracted men the way she did.

"Toni, I'm thrilled someone else has an interest in you. I don't know why you feel obligated to stay with him. You don't seem happy. There are tons of men who would give anything to have you," Jelly said.

Darius was choosing a CD from Toni's collection, and never looked away from the stereo.

"Is Raymond nice? Who is he?" Darius queried.

Toni blushed. She was somewhat smitten by the attention from Raymond.

"He is an executive for the Houston Ballet. He's been an acquaintance for several years. We have never been very close, but I've always found him attractive. He seems very interested in me, and I see he hasn't made any advances out of respect for Jon. Obviously somebody told him Jon is no longer an issue. I'm actually glad because I want to date other people. I have mentioned that fact to Jon, hoping he would step up his game. I get tired of coaching Jon on the next move. I need a friend in whom I can confide, with whom I can share ideas and especially someone who can appreciate a weekend getaway at the spur of the moment just to relax.

"Recently, he has been making excuses not to go, so I don't ask anymore. I need some change and some spice, and food isn't what I have in mind. I'm just tired of the excitement in my life being the last movie I saw alone; the last book I read, alone; the last banquet, ball, and the last social event, I attended alone. He could never go anywhere with me and my best friends as a group. His insecurity overwhelms me. I'm done," Toni sighed, as she relaxed in her leather chair and sipped her champagne.

"The best thing is to end it, to continue to be his friend and move on. He really should be out of the picture before you start dating," Darius said.

"Besides I don't think you should date Raymond. I really like Dr. Morris. He seems very interested in you. He also understands your demanding schedule, which will make him appreciate your time. He'll understand the need to make the private moments you two enjoy very special. He is also extremely intellectual, and equally passionate about the same things you are."

Toni raised an eyebrow at Darius as he finished.

"I talked to him for a while during the party. I believe you two would have a wonderful, intense relationship. My vote is for Dr. Morris," Darius chuckled, as he picked up a pen and a piece of paper and drew a ballot listing Dr. Morris, Raymond and Jon's names. He marked the box in front of Dr. Morris's name, folded it and handed it to

Toni. She laughed until she nearly cried.

As they unwrapped boxes, Toni realized she had some things to do. It was all about timing now. She decided to wait until they went out of town before making her final decision. She wanted to make the right one. Jon had been in her life a long time. She needed to be certain that Dr. Morris realized he was not transitional. She didn't want Raymond or anyone else to feel that way, either.

"By the way, Jackie got prices for a trip to Aspen around Christmas. I think we should go then. Before Thanksgiving is going to stretch me but I'm sure I can swing it. The rates weren't that different between the two holidays. She checked Vail as well. She obtained some brochures, and Aspen seems to be more our style. It seems more quiet and relaxed. The brochures also stated that instructors provide more personal attention. The other option is to go to Aspen first, and then to Vail on the next holiday. I would love that. I just want to ski."

"Let me get my calendar out of our car. I'm game for both dates, if you two are. I'll be right back." Darius's easy stride and long legs put him at the door in an instant. Jelly followed to get her own planner.

They returned and Jelly sat in the recliner crossing her legs. She was usually game to do exciting things, so it was no surprise when she agreed that they travel to both destinations.

"It's been a long time since we all took a trip together. It's been two years since we went to New Orleans. I had an excellent time, but I'd like to go somewhere new and different. This is great." Jelly had resolved within herself that this was indeed the most promising vacation that she had heard of in a long time. She looked at dates for December's trip.

"Okay, Toni. I'll agree to both trips," Darius agreed. "Let's talk about December dates. Let's go to Aspen first. I suggest leaving December the 26 and returning December 30 or January 2. This all depends on where you want to spend New Year's Eve and day." Darius would think of these details Toni thought to herself.

"Well, it's settled. We'll be going to both. I'll have Jackie purchase the tickets and make the hotel arrangements. Knowing Jackie, she'll probably already have a list of suggested items to take on a ski trip. I'll ask her to research the ski slope options as well. You know how thorough Jackie is. I'm looking at leaving Tuesday or Wednesday before Thanksgiving and returning on Sunday or Monday. How's that for you two?" Toni flipped through her calendar for the exact dates.

"Are you bringing Martin? You've been seeing each other awhile." Darius questioned.

"Are you bringing Julia?" Jelly laughed, knowing that he had been avoiding her serious advances.

"I can't go with Jon," Toni said. "I'll have to spend ten days with him. I'm going to tell him that the three of us are going alone. I don't know anyone that well right now. Maybe Philip could go. As a matter of fact, I think I'll call him now." She moved off the sofa to get the phone, and paged him.

Toni answered the phone in the kitchen. "Hello."

"Hello, Toni. How are you?"

"I'm almost recuperated from the party. How are you?"

"I'm well. I enjoyed your party. It was really nice. I love your house. I would like to sit down with Darius and talk about having him work up some plans for the home I'm going to build."

"I can give you his number so you two can get together."

"That would be great. We talked for a few minutes at your house. I forgot why I was there." She could tell he was blushing over the phone.

"Do you ski?" She paused for his answer.

"Sure, why do you ask?" Eager for her response.

"Well, I called because we are planning a ski trip and I wondered if you wanted to join me?" She closed her eyes. She hadn't been this nervous since high school when she was waiting to hear if she was the school's queen.

Philip was slow to respond. "I would be glad to join you."

"Well, great," Toni said.

"Do I need to help plan or anything?" Philip seemed eager at this point.

"No, my assistant will make all of the arrangements and I'll fax them to you. My travel agent found a real nice secluded resort. Anyway, I'm glad you're able to come."

"I'm glad too. I'm looking forward to this trip. Toni, I would really like to see you before then. How about dinner later this week?" Philip was truly glad Toni had called. He wanted to be with this wonderful woman, and hoped this would be the beginning of a healthy relationship. He enjoyed the party and felt much more comfortable with Toni. Before, it seemed, she had put up a wall between them. He also noticed some distance between she and Jon when she introduced them. He put the dates in his planner and made a note to call Jackie so he could make some arrangements of his own. This trip would be unforgettable.

"Sure. This week is fine." Now Toni was blushing.

"I'll talk to you tomorrow. Thanks for calling."

As she entered the entertainment room, "Well, the discussion about my date is over. Dr. Philip Morris will be accompanying me to Aspen. I didn't realize how excited I would be, but I'm truly excited he accepted my invitation." Toni said, closing her planner. She lay back on the leather couch and exhaled. She sipped champagne and absorbed the music.

Darius was still making notes in his planner. Jelly flipped through magazines. "We'll get together on the Christmas plans once we get the Aspen details complete. We don't want to overburden Jackie," Darius said, but smiling at Jelly. Toni simply raised her hand, but her eyes were still closed.

Chapter eight

"Good morning, Dr. T. Sorry to disturb you, but I believe these are for you." Kiki stepped aside as a delivery person placed a huge floral arrangement on the conference table. Toni thanked and tipped the driver. She opened the card fully expecting it to read 'from Jon,' his usual card, with nothing creative.

She was surprised when the card read, "Sorry I couldn't make your reception. Looking forward to seeing you, soon. Sincerely, Arthur." He included his mobile number on the business card. Toni was impressed. She had no idea he was interested in her. He was friends with her attorney. She knew very little about his personal life. She did know he was a successful attorney.

She was sending an e-mail when the door opened again. This time Jen brought another delivery person with two-dozen sterling roses. Toni was beginning to become concerned. This was bouquet number two, and it was still before 10 a.m. The card read: 'Dinner for two. Monday at 6 p.m. Please. Sincerely, Philip.' Toni blushed.

Just when she had gained her composure, Jackie walked in with packages in hand, Toni's gifts to the staff for their dedication. It made Toni so happy to give her friends things they adored and would enjoy over the years. Jackie distributed the boxes with a disapproving glance to Toni. Then, one of the other receptionists accepted a third arrangement of flowers for Toni. Toni pointed him to the writing table. She pulled the card as he walked by, and tipped him on the way out.

"Finally, flowers from Jon." Toni sighed and placed the card on her desk.

Jackie was well into the package by then and the others followed her lead. Jackie read the thank you card from Toni, then the invitation. As a thank you, Toni had extended a dinner invitation to each staff member. A sheer ribbon secured the gold invitation. When Jackie saw the crystal jewelry box, she gasped. She had seen it one day when she and Toni were shopping for office furnishings.

Kiki beat Daphne by a squeal. She put on her beaded bracelet and nearly squashed Daphne in an attempt thank Toni. Daphne viewed her elephant as a parent would a precious newborn. Toni had seen it circled in a catalog.

Toni made Kiki's bracelet by hand, and later Kiki let Toni know that she was aware. Finally, Jen made it to her gift. Jen received a gift certificate for a custom-made wedding veil. Toni had overheard Jen tell Kiki that the wedding budget wasn't as large as it needed to be, so Toni paid for her veil and other accessories that she would receive when she selected her veil. Jen cried. They all tried to hug Toni at once. Their hug was interrupted when Darius knocked on the door with a box in hand. "Thanks, again, Dr. T." Her staff closed the door behind them.

Darius, still holding his box, noticed the flowers. "Did someone die or is someone greatly loved?" He noticed the cards at the edge of her desk.

She chuckled because of the cards, but more importantly because she knew what his box contained. It was an engraved business card holder, and a gift certificate to Ruggles, his favorite restaurant. It also held a claim check for an autographed print by John Biggers for his new office.

"Let's go to lunch, lady. I'm sure Jackie can let you slip away for an hour."

Jackie entered and signaled for Toni to answer the phone.

"Yes, Jelly."

"You are incredible. You manage to do this to me every time. I opened that box and the vase was beautiful. You know that I love you. I'm hugging you right now. I'm nearly crying, too. But, I've got to go." Jelly could hardly hang up the phone without sniffling. Although, Toni knew how emotional Jelly was, she didn't anticipate this response. If she had known, she would've selected a more personal way of presenting it to her.

Darius had checked with Jackie while Toni was on the phone. He decided to wait while Toni saw her one appointment before lunch. It was a simple check-up, then they were off.

♦ ♦ ♦ ♦ ♦

"I invited you here as a token of my appreciation for you. Not because of what you do but because of who you are to me."

"So, I would like to propose a toast: "To your good health, God's will, protection and guidance in your life and success with your heart's desires."

"I'm very grateful to have each of you in my life."

The caterer had worked diligently to accommodate Toni's requests. Toni even made crab cakes for an appetizer.

They moved on to the entrée with a crisp Riesling wine. Toni served a lightly herbed crusted smoked salmon fillet, with green beans and dill potatoes.
"Dinner was wonderful." Jackie spoke for the group. She closed with a phenomenal flambé dessert and chocolate cake, with coffee and hot tea. "That was good. I'm going to need a piece of that to go." Darius tried to hide the crumbs he dropped as he walked. Toni burst into laughter, "Yes, you may." She had already prepared take-home desserts for everyone. Finally, she placed a small purple box at each table setting holding a chocolate covered, long-stem strawberry. "Life doesn't get anymore
complete than this. Thank you. Each of you bless my life. I only hope that I'm half the blessing you are to me. Thank you for being in my life. Thank you. To-go desserts are in the kitchen." Toni wiped the single tear that slid down her face.

Chapter nine

"Dang, Jackie come on. We've got to work out these details for Toni's surprise birthday party. We've got to call Jon, Jelly and Darius to be sure we have what we need. Okay, did you get the keys to the house out of her drawer?" Kiki always got nervous when they tried to surprise Toni.

Daphne was keeping her late on rounds so she would get back to the office late.

Jackie had Toni's cleaning delivered late as well. Toni usually got home by eight, so she had planned to change clothes at the office. Jon was meeting her at 8:30 p.m. Toni thought they were going to dinner at Anthony's.

Jen met Jackie to let the caterer into the house. Jelly met them to finish decorating.

Jon parked his Volvo in the circle drive just minutes before Toni's BMW turned the corner. He grabbed Toni's mail so she could place it inside. He had to pull this off. He should've let Darius do it. Toni was simply stubborn. He remembered the key to success was her dry cleaning and hoping that she wouldn't let up the garage door.

Toni hoped out of the car and rushed to the door. She apologized to Jon for being late, and said she would only be a minute. Jon took her keys and opened the front door.

"SURPRISE!" Everyone yelled at the top of their lungs. Toni was in awe.

She hugged Jon, then Darius and Jelly. Jackie and Kiki made their way over to her. Then Daphne came with plates in hand. They seated Toni so she could feast on the wonderful hors d'oeuvres.

Toni admired their hard work in planning this event, and wondered how much Jon had to do with it.

After the appetizers, she thanked each guest individually. She soon learned that dancing had been planned on the evening's agenda. Some of the same faces were there from the housewarming party. She mingled a little more, then Philip asked could they dance but didn't wait for an answer as he whisked her off to the dance floor. She didn't leave the floor for an hour. She had several partners, each accompanied by a present and a new glass of champagne. She just kept dancing, and they kept coming. The party ended around two in the morning, which was a good thing, because she had worn out her shoes.

♦ ♦ ♦ ♦ ♦

They arrived in Atlanta around noon, and ate at the hotel's café. They stayed in Atlanta overnight so that could tour the Martin Luther King exhibits, and the museums along with some shopping.

His home was first. It was a cozy two-story. The authenticity of the items in the house was excellent. The original style washer was still there. Toni did not believe the games in the family room were original, though the quilts on the bed appeared authentic. She owned one similar to the one on the daughter's bed.

She was impressed with the preservation. They had made some modifications for tourism purposes, of course, such as central air and heat, some additional stairs and some safety effects. Overall, however, the home seemed to be in better than original condition. Toni was surprised that the homes surrounding the King's were still occupied. It was like a tourist attraction within a neighborhood.

The next stop was the gallery and monument. The gallery continued excellent pictures of Dr. King. There were several photos of him with Coretta, and one with the children. There were two rooms with different personal effects including clothes, old cologne bottles, an old Bible, his pastoral garb and some furniture. Toni also saw the dress Coretta wore to her husband's funeral.

The second room's theme depicted his political activity. There were pictures and articles about King and Ghandi, both taken in India. There were a couple of Ghandi alone. Both men had published books, which were also on display. Dr. King's speeches were in a display case along with his magnifying glass and some reading glasses. He was photographed with Lyndon Baines Johnson and Jimmy Carter after receiving the Nobel Peace Prize. An interesting latchhook design of Dr. King hung on the wall.

"I wonder if the person who painted the canvas was the same person who did the latchhook."

"That's an interesting observation."

She let out a shallow gasp when she saw the tomb centered on the water with flags lining the walkway overhead. The pool was about seventy-five feet long. They took several photos of the site. As they neared the end of the pool, she gawked, "Are they tanning on the memorial?"

Jon remained silent.

Next on their agenda was Ebenezer Baptist Church, which had also remained intact. It still had the mahogany furnishings with the deep burgundy seat cushions and drapes. The sun streamed through the stained-glass windows so there was no need for lights.

Toni studied the ministers' photos on the wall. She paid particular attention to Dr. King, Sr. He reminded her of her maternal great-grandfather. She paused for a moment, and said a short prayer.

Jon watched Toni's every move. He adored her and all of her attributes, thinking that she was gorgeous. He knew that it was almost over–he remembered the look in her eyes when she danced with other men who found her attractive. He decided to make the best of this trip.

Toni wandered around touching items wondering how dynamic it must have been to sit in his presence. She finally finished and wandered out where Jon was sitting. Next, they tooled around 'The Underground,' and bought a few post cards, magnets and T-shirts as souvenirs.

Toni enjoyed flying. She sunk into her seat and started writing. Her writing had been neglected lately. She looked over at Jon. He was already asleep, and they had only been airborne for thirty minutes. She was somewhat relieved to have time to write. This was the quiet time she envisioned. The flight attendant continued to serve champagne throughout the flight. Toni kept writing and sipping.

When they arrived in Grand Cayman, Toni took a nap, and afterwards felt completely renewed. They savored surf and turf at the captain's table on the dinner cruise.

Gambling was also part of the entertainment on the boat. And of course, Jon couldn't wait to try his luck. Toni was only slightly interested, but she did play blackjack. Jon played craps. With $500 to her credit, she moved on the slots. She only stayed a short while and moved with an additional $250 to her credit. Jon was nearly ready to give up when he hit it big. He stepped away from the table with $750. He found Toni at another 21 table. They returned to their stateroom with $2000 to their credit.

They requested that dessert be served in the room. They celebrated their winning with fresh strawberries and ice cream and chocolate cake.

The highlight of the next day was the scuba diving. They took lessons for forty-five minutes, then dove for the next two hours. Toni had borrowed an underwater camera from one of her colleagues. She got some excellent shots. The dive was quite strenuous which would explain why the concierge had scheduled a massage following the dive, where Toni fell asleep.

They spent the following day hiking, so Jon arranged to have dinner brought to the room. The circular bay window overlooked the beach. Romantic. He had outdone himself.

When Toni entered the room, she focused on the fish in a crystal bowl surrounded by candles. The salad decorated the table. Jon stood tableside pouring white wine in her glass. Toni also noticed a bouquet of flowers on the windowsill.

Jon placed the wine back in the chiller. He held out his hand so she could step down to the table. She was seated and they prayed. She sliced her ribeye to check the temperature. Perfect. Toni was amazed at the effort Jon had expended to entertain her.

Jon then brought out a small birthday cake bearing her name and one purple candle. He changed the jazz disc to a tape where her staff, her friends and Jon sang the Stevie Wonder happy birthday tune. She laughed in surprise.

Toni figured that since he had gone to the bedroom and it was close to his bedtime, she thought the evening had ended and she was prepared to write for a while. She was comfortable on the sofa when the suite's doorbell rang. She looked over her shoulder hoping the bell hadn't disturbed Jon. She opened the door and the waiter presented her with a covered silver tray and a rolling champagne chiller. She placed it on the bar. She returned to tip the waiter but he had disappeared. She went back to the bar, raised the cover and found a note with four chocolate-covered strawberries inside.

Onedia N. Gage  51

The note read:

"Dear Toni,

Leave your notebook and laptop on the table. You won't need them. Bring the tray to the bathroom.

Love, Jon."

She smiled, and slipped off her shoes. She moved her laptop to the desk, and picked up the tray. As she walked, she was led by a trail of rose petals to the dressing area where Jon was waiting by the Jacuzzi bath with more rose petals, another champagne chiller, and two full glasses with fresh strawberries on the rims.

There was another full bowl of strawberries on a tray with chocolates and sugar, as well as another bottle of champagne on the counter. She was impressed with Jon's thoroughness. He then guided her to the tub.

"Enjoy your bath," Jon said, leaving to give her privacy. Once outside, he leaned on the doorframe and signed heavily. He was so afraid of losing her.

Toni walked out of the bathroom, and Jon was asleep. Or at least he pretended to be. She wondered what was happening.

Jon awoke as a new man. He was encouraged that Toni had cooperated last evening, but worried that she was becoming bored with him. He didn't do this type of thing often. He sat there admiring her as she slept. He realized that he had to regroup to become the man she needed. Until now, he had been confused. He thought she didn't need a man. But now, after a 6-day vacation, he realized that she needed a man to love her intimately, to support and encourage her, and to be her soul mate. Jon did not know if he could be that man.

♦♦♦♦♦

Toni stood on the cliff and looked at the sparkling ocean below. As her instructor, Ken said, "It was time to "jump and glide." She gave her thumbs up, then soared into the air. Her take-off was excellent. Adrenaline pumped through her body. She felt as light as a butterfly. She had always wanted to do this but never had the opportunity. She admired the sun and the water and could almost see other islands from here. She turned gently and headed toward the landing spot and landed perfectly. She looked as if she just walked out of the air.

"Can I go again? I really liked it. It was more than I imagined. I am so pumped," Toni asked, looking back and forth between Jon and the instructor. Toni didn't realize that repeat performances were unprecedented. Further, she didn't realize she was the only one jumping. A group of people had gathered to observe. She thought they were jumpers, as well, until they walked back to their shuttle bus.

Her instructor shook his head as he removed her gear. "Toni, is it? I have another class. You were the only one on schedule. Those people may glide later, but they were observing. What I will do is to have your account credited because I can't allow you to jump again today. I also don't want you to rearrange your schedule for the following days to try to reschedule your jump. But, I will give you the names of some groups and instructors so you can go gliding in the States. Where are you from?"

"Houston. I may need to come back. This is something that I've always wanted to do and it just didn't last long enough." Toni followed Ken back to the shuttle trying to figure out when she would be able to do this again. All of a sudden, thoughts of Philip filled her psyche. "This trip just got too long," she thought.

The balloon ride did a little to satisfy Toni's need for adventure compared to the hang gliding. The countryside was breathtaking. The other islands appeared even smaller. The sun rose as they were on their ascent. It was so colorful and magnificent, Godly. She was so moved, she almost forgot to take pictures. They moved so fluidly through the air. Toni inhaled deeply. The air was so fresh and clean. They traveled about an hour before they started their descent.

Back on the ground, they toasted with champagne, and strawberries. This week's diet. But breakfast was not complete until they enjoyed buttermilk pancakes with warm maple syrup, chicken strips, and freshly squeezed grapefruit juice outside on the patio. A 60-year old husband and wife team, who had lived on the island for about fifteen years, owned the balloons and a bed and breakfast. The two couples talked for another hour afterwards. The husband drove she and Jon back to the hotel and presented them with a souvenir bottle of champagne and the landing photo of their journey.

When they arrived in Miami, Toni immediately experienced Grand Cayman withdrawal. Jon noticed her facial expression and just chuckled.

"That fresh air got you, huh?" Jon jested.

"Yeah that and my luggage is heavier than before because of all that shopping. I was supposed to mail some of this stuff. I'll do it tomorrow." She sighed.

♦ ♦ ♦ ♦ ♦

"I'm glad we're staying the night in Kentucky," Jon commented, thinking the more time the better.

Kentucky's countryside was more picturesque than usual. In addition to getting lost, the cab driver was impersonating Mario Andretti. Toni wanted to remind him that they were not at the Indy 500, but Jon kept whispering in her ear and making her laugh.

When they arrived at the ranch, she and Rita caught up on the latest news, while Jon and Jorge brought the luggage inside the house. Rita had already prepared chicken and fresh avocado on wheat, with honey mustard and all of the trimmings. She seated Toni and Jon and served the sandwiches with homemade pasta salad, chips, and fresh pink lemonade.

Toni decided to nap before riding. Cocoa, her mare, would be excited to see her. She hadn't been to Kentucky to ride in a while. She had owned Cocoa for nearly 10 years. She elected to keep the house and ranch in tact. She received at least a dozen phone calls to sell, but she always said no. Rita and Jorge had worked for her grandfather as long as she could remember. She had spent every summer here.

When she woke, Jon was sitting across the room in her rocker reading a book. She could count the number of times she had seen him reading. She sat up in the bed and asked him to share. He was reading a relationship book by a husband-wife team. She had read it and inspired him to do so as well.

"Hey, I want to answer the quizzes with you. I'm finding this really interesting."

"Okay," she replied carefully. She wondered where all of this was coming from. If she had asked him to do that, he would've ignored her. She was minimally impressed with his effort, yet still confused about his motivation.

Cocoa was an 11-year old cinnamon-colored mare. Toni never understood the horse age calculation; not to mention the dog age calculation.

Toni had a very relaxing ride. She and Cocoa traveled at least 2 1/2 miles. As they circled the lake, thoughts of fishing crept into her mind.

Just as she turned the last corner, Toni saw Jon walking Mister, a jet-black stallion.

"Wanna ride?" Jon pulled her up after he mounted.

Cocoa roamed in the training arena while she and Jon then rode Mister together for about a mile.

"Let's walk back." Jon took her hand in his. "Can we leave early in the morning?"

"Is there something wrong?" Toni responded trying to conceal her shock.

"We haven't been the best in years. I can't continue to hold you and not satisfy you." Jon stopped and looked into her eyes.

She saw hurt and confusion, but knew this was best. "We'll always be friends. Thank you for my birthday."

"I hope we make better friends. I will miss you." He turned toward the lake.

She rested her hand on his back to comfort him, "If we are to be together, we will. Right now, it's not that time. We should've addressed this realistically a few weeks ago. And I am to blame for that."

"If you need anything, be sure to call." He replied, turning to face her again.

"Thanks."

They ambled back towards the barn. He didn't release her hand until they were standing in front of the training area.

Rita and Jorge looked sad when she announced that they were leaving early. "I'll be back before Christmas," Toni gently reminded them. She and Jon bid them farewell as the cab took them to the airport.

Since they arrived home two days earlier than planned, Toni didn't really know what to do with herself. She decided to work on Friday and until noon on Saturday. She stayed home on Thursday to write.

She sat in her bay window and thought to herself. Her relationship with Jon was over. She had to admit she was somewhat saddened, yet relieved. She exhaled and closed her eyes.

Chapter ten

"The Galleria, right?" Toni asked, as if she shopped anywhere else. She did, however, shop at Baybrook and Memorial City malls and occasionally went to Town & Country.

Jelly shook her head in approval knowing that this was no time to argue with Toni about where to go. Had she been on time, Toni would have been more apt to listen. Right now they just needed to get to a mall.

Toni and Jelly were mostly silent on the ride there. Jelly decided she needed to complete her list and become serious about this. Toni was not to be challenged when she became focused on a task.

Toni parked near Lord & Taylor. She wanted to run by Crate & Barrel and Macy's first. Once they began shopping, Toni decided to talk. They hadn't really talked in a while.

"Jelly, Jon and I are not seeing each other anymore. We left Kentucky a day early and cut the trip short by two days. We both felt it was best. It will be different spending the holidays without him," Toni sighed. She realized that she had spoken the words for the first time since making them final.

Jelly stopped to hug her. "Jelly, that's all I have to say about that," Toni said, wiping a single tear from her cheek. Jelly knew to wait until Toni was ready to discuss it again.

"What do you think about Philip?" Toni questioned Jelly.

"I like him. He seems extremely nice, somewhat reserved, yet genuinely interested in you. Are you still inviting him to Aspen?" Jelly asked.

"Yes, I like him, and he's already agreed to go to Aspen. I'll need to shop for that trip while we're here. Don't you need some things too?" Toni asked.

"Just a few things. You know I've been skiing twice since the last time you went."

"We've got to move faster. I have a date with Philip tonight."

She finally responded to the dinner invitation he extended before her birthday. She had called Friday from the office to let him know that she was home. He asked her out for this evening, so she suggested that the date was her treat. Although she had wonderful intentions, he halted her advances. He said, "I'll be there at eight. I'm wearing khaki pants, a cotton shirt and loafers." When she hung up the phone, her stomach fluttered, just as it had when she first saw him.

"I'm glad you are moving on with your life. You know I'm here for you." Jelly spoke barely above a whisper.

In the next three hours, they completed their lists, and settled in for a leisurely lunch at a restaurant in the mall. Toni had slowed down, and her list had grown. She looked down at all the packages and wished she had valet parked. Toni really enjoyed Jelly's company. They were midway through lunch when they spotted Darius.

"Julia, there's Toni and Jelly."

Toni greeted Darius with a hug. She extended her hand to Julia. "How are you?"

"Fine. I forgot about this traffic." Julia spoke in a warm voice.

"It's nice to see you." Jelly extended her hand to Julia.

"How long has she been torturing you?" Darius chimed in teasing Jelly.

Toni playfully punched him in the arm. "Would you care to join us?" Toni turned to Julia.

"No, thank you. We'll wait." Darius replied.

"Jelly, we need to go to the ski store. I almost forgot."

"Girl, I'm tired. I don't see how you do it." "See you guys later." Jelly and Toni said as they departed for the mall.

A beautiful, salt-water fish tank surrounded the booth in the restaurant. The setting was almost too romantic.

"Toni, I'm glad you agreed to have dinner with me. I've been thinking about you a lot. I'd like to see more of you. Forgive me for being so direct, but I know no other way. I need you to know how I feel and what my intentions are." Philip smiled, shyly.

She knew he was genuine. She knew at that moment she wanted him in her life. She felt his sensitivity and care. She knew almost from the start that he would meet her needs.

"I'm interested in spending more time with you, as well. That's why I invited you to Aspen. I feel that you are sincere." Toni stated.

"How was your birthday? Your office told me you were out of town." Philip spoke slowly.

"The trip was beautiful. The Caymans were extraordinary. I would really like to revisit Grand Cayman and, of course, I go to Kentucky regularly. Jon and I ended our relationship." Toni twisted her hair. "I thought of you. I'm looking forward to our trip to Aspen."

"Just like that? It ended?" Philip probed.

"You just know. It was over long before the words were ever uttered. Can we talk about something else?"

"Sure. I missed you." Philip had her hands cupped inside his. This was one of those times when her petite stature was obvious. His hands completely covered hers. His eyes met hers. She was in love. Philip was a perfect gentleman. After dinner he and the valet helped her into the Land Cruiser. They talked for hours at the edge of the park's waterfall. They ended their evening at her front door where he pulled her close for a long, intimate kiss. She did not want to leave his warm embrace. He was on cloud nine. He was so enthralled with her entire being.

Chapter eleven

Thanksgiving was extra special. This was the first time that her great-grandfather had walked alone in several years. He even smiled when she picked him up at the retirement home. Since the strokes and the onset of cancer and arthritis, everything had been difficult for him. His doctor thought that he might be developing Alzheimer's disease, as well. So much had happened to his frail body.

It was hard for her to see him in this shape. After all, this was the man who had taught her to cook, and to fish. He even combed her hair. She saw him every other weekend. They spoiled her until her great-grandmother died. From her death, his health began to deteriorate.

He had no one to take care of now. The love of his life had died. His great-granddaughter was growing up. He had lost his will to live. When she saw him moving by himself, she was overwhelmed. Now, she was convinced that he would come to Kentucky with her in two weeks. He had agreed to go to Kentucky but they weren't sure he would get medical clearance. She thought he might even fly.

Her mother was so excited to see "Papa." Her mother had just arrived with her husband, whom Toni affectionately called Dad. They blessed the food and served hors d'oeuvres and punch. Jelly and Darius greeted everyone. She had everything catered except the cornbread dressing, which she made herself. She was determined to master the recipe before her grandmother passed away. Cornbread dressing was her favorite part of Thanksgiving dinner. She also taught the caterer how to make the potato salad just the way the family liked it. She presented it to the connoisseurs and critics, better known as her mother and grandmother, and it passed with flying colors.

Toni had left some instructions behind: one of which was that her staff and her family be seated. The caterers were being paid to serve them, she reminded them.

Her grandmother seemed miffed, "I don't know why we couldn't cook and you had to hire this caterer."

Toni whispered in her grandmother's ear, "If I had let you cook, I would not be able to sit next to you to whisper in your ear. I have never sat next to you at dinner." Toni sat between her great-grandfather and her grandmother, with her mother directly across from her.

Dinner was everything she planned. She served sweet potato pie, pound cake, and pecan pie, both topped with ice cream. She had made them herself, and a chocolate cake, which the caterer made. They talked for a while before Toni left to take her great-grandfather back to his nursing home. She wanted him to stay but she had not planned for that. When her great-grandfather hugged her at the house after dinner, she started crying. She had to turn her back so he wouldn't see her tears.

Philip rode with her to drop him to the home. The nurse came in and asked them both to leave so that he could take his medicine. Toni kissed him on the forehead and a single tear dropped on his hand. He looked up to find her face wet. He wiped the left side with his hand then reached for the right with his handkerchief. He patted her on the arm and said good-bye. Outside in the hallway Philip knelt in front of her and put her forehead on his. He rubbed her shoulders then kissed her on the forehead. Her sobs quieted by that point. The ride back was somber.

She slumped into her favorite chair. She didn't realize that Jelly, Darius and her mother were still there. Philip was talking quietly to them in the kitchen. She met them at the door and hugged each one.

"Thanks for dinner, Toni." Jelly spoke and Darius nodded in agreement.

"You're welcome. Mom, call me when you get home, please."

Philip stayed with her for about another hour. They didn't speak. He rubbed her feet. Then he moved her to the sofa where he rubbed her back. She had long since stopped crying, but she was still sad. She didn't realize that this could be that hard on her. She let Philip out the door and took a nap. She had a couple of days to pack and prepare for Aspen.

♦ ♦ ♦ ♦ ♦

Promptly at seven on Sunday morning, Philip rang the doorbell. Toni was almost ready. They were going to church and then return home to eat Thanksgiving leftovers. They also wanted to shop for more gear for the trip. She had gotten up extremely early because of the time she retired. She had nearly completed packing. They were scheduled to leave Wednesday. She had a staff meeting on Monday and a tight appointment schedule for the next two days.

Once in the office on Monday, the staff meeting was forty-five minutes away but she reviewed several items with Jackie first.

"These are the balances in all accounts, including the payroll account on the last page. With the exception of that account, I have printed the activity since November 1st. The balances are at the bottom of each page. Your credit cards are listed on the last page, only two have balances. You used one for shopping and then the other for the office. The activity for those purchases are also included. The office one lists activity since the last payment was made," Jackie explained, handing her the pages for review.

Toni took the pages. She started with her cards. She glanced over the page for her personal expenses and handed it back to Jackie. Then she asked for it back.

"Jackie, where did you put the Aspen trip. It's not listed here. Are the charges not applied yet? The plane tickets should be on here already."

Jackie produced a folder, almost from behind her back. She had been afraid to tell Toni what happened. Toni took the folder from Jackie. She looked in the folder and pulled out the documents. She saw the tickets for Jelly, with a photocopy of a check, with a name that she didn't recognize immediately, which was Jelly's guest. Then she came to it.

There were two charge slips, tickets and a voided receipt attached to the tickets. The charge tickets and the voided receipt had her name on them. The third slip had no signature and she couldn't find a name immediately. She kept looking from the ticket to Jackie, but Jackie had her head down. Finally, she focused and found the name: "P.J. Morris." She looked up at Jackie with her mouth open.

"Jackie, what happened here?"

"When his assistant called, he asked for the name of our travel agent. He wanted all the information just like I gave everyone else. To make a long story short. When the tickets arrived, the agent had followed our instructions, but there were some changes. I called the agency and they told me Dr. Morris had called to charge the expenses himself. He paid for the tickets, the hotel arrangements, the lessons package and lift coupons. He upgraded your room to a two-bedroom suite. When he called to tell me what he did, I was worried what your response would be, so I thought that I would let him explain. I'm really sorry. I hope that you're not mad."

"Jackie, I'm not upset. I'm not even concerned that he did this. I'm surprised because he hadn't said anything. I'm flattered. I'll act surprised. You handled it well, as usual. I simply wondered why it wasn't on my charge card." Toni smiled at his surprise.

"You can pay my personal card, then do the same with the office card. How are collections with insurance coming?"

"The insurance companies are paying within sixty days without extra effort. I only have one at ninety days, but I should have it clear soon. It's sixty dollars."

"Well, the trip arrangements look real good. I'm looking forward to it. I'm all packed. Thank you for helping me with this. We're going to have a great time. That must be the caterer. It's 2:30 p.m. Okay, let's get set up. I need the schedule for the week I return."

The attendant's voice rang out clear as a bell announcing that all passengers traveling first class to Aspen and Denver should board from the left side.

Jelly's guest, Martin, tried to calm her and entertain her until the door opened. Darius's guest, Julia, was excited, too.

They were served salmon and champagne. Toni had brought several books and kept them by her side. When Toni finally decided to read, the plane was due to land in thirty minutes.

When Toni was finally able to see beyond the clouds she admired the beautiful snow-capped mountains. She had never seen Colorado from above. This view was awesome. The last time she was in Denver, they drove.

When they arrived at the hotel, it was everything she imagined. When Darius and Jelly got to their rooms, they each called Toni to thank her for the fruit basket she sent. Jelly felt bad. Toni always does this.

Toni simply loved the suite Philip selected. The room had French doors at the entrance. There was a foyer with a round table inside with a huge, fresh bouquet. Off to the left was a bedroom, further up the hallway there was a dining room with entryways between the kitchen and the secluded living area. In the bedroom on the right, was the sunken Jacuzzi bath. There were fireplaces in the living area and the bedrooms. It held such romantic promises.

Philip came out of his room with a card addressed to him that was previously attached to a basket. "Come here, you. You never cease to amaze me." He put the card in his pocket and rubbed noses with Toni.

"I can't wait until tomorrow. I'm so excited about skiing." She hugged him and buried her head in his chest.

"I'm excited too. The instructor will be here after lunch to inspect our equipment."

That evening, when they returned to their rooms, Toni and Philip shared an intimate candlelight dinner, starting with red bean soup. They ate the best steak in all of Colorado accompanied by pasta and a vegetable medley, with a crisp red wine. The dessert was pecan pie with ice cream, Philip's favorite. The fireplace had been lit in the living room where she read her poetry to him. He read Nikki Giovanni's poetry to her. They drank more white wine after dessert. They read to one another until they both drifted off to sleep. They were sleeping in each other's arms when the doorbell disturbed them. They almost missed the casino trip with the others. Toni was not impressed with the casino, yet she left with the largest amount of winnings.

By the third day of skiing, the eve before their departure, they all skied the more difficult slopes. Toni was a little nervous. She had grasped the skills quite quickly, though. She had built her confidence because of her success on the easier slopes. They were all doing really well.

That evening, she and Philip had a private dinner in their suite. "What is this?" Philip questioned.

"Just a few things I had prepared for you." Toni responded coyly. Toni had arranged for his favorite meal to be prepared. They had crab cakes to start and a salad. The chef had prepared Beef Wellington. Philip's mouth watered when he saw the plate. He wondered how she knew.

"I guess you did some homework, too," alluding to his earlier surprises.

"I just wanted to give you some of your favorite things."

"Thank you. I'm speechless. And just like you, that's rare."

"You're not supposed to say anything. I just want you to enjoy. Are you ready for dessert?" The dessert was cherries flambé.

"I have to be in heaven. Pinch me." He held out his arm in front of her. She laughed heartily. "Dinner was great. To what do I owe the privilege?"

"Just being you—warm, attentive and special. The evening's not over yet. Come." She led him to her room, where she massaged his back. They spent some quiet time together lying on her bed.

"What makes you so peaceful?" Philip probed.

"My spiritual life is first. Then, I ask myself how important is that— whatever excited me or frustrated me. Is all of that anger and anguish worth it? When I realized that, I became a lot more peaceful. What makes you so reserved?"

"I've seen a lot. The loss of my father. The loss of others. Surgery shows me a lot about people. Their priorities change on that table. And when they don't come off of that table, I'm reminded that life is too short for nonsense."

"That is true indeed. Most people find out too late how short life really is." Toni agreed.

♦ ♦ ♦ ♦ ♦

Jelly hosted the group in the main dining room for breakfast. Jelly started, "Good morning. We have had a good time. We have skied, shopped, eaten, rested and slept. Everyone raise your glasses. I'll go first. I am thankful for the thoughtful persons in my life, especially for the diva in my life, Ms. Antoinette Harden."

They each toasted to their friendships. Their guests joined in as well, making some very warm comments.

Philip was last to speak. He stood, cleared his throat and turned to Toni. "You are extremely special to me. I have been on cloud nine since I awarded you that vase a few months ago. In a very short time, you have captured my heart, and my soul. You have taken me by storm. I want to thank you for the impact you have had on me. On top of that, you are so inspirational. Thank you."

As he sat down, Jelly approached her with a box. "This is a material representation of our thanks and love." While she hugged Jelly in appreciation, Toni was wondering why the breakfast had been focused on her.

They insisted that she open the box. She picked the dainty necklace up and found a diamond cross at the end. She placed her hand over her mouth in surprise. She had mentioned to Jelly that she wanted this piece while they were out shopping.

She caught Philip attempting to slide another box her way. "This is from me," Philip spoke slowly. Once inside, she found a pair of diamond stud earrings and a diamond tennis bracelet. She was overwhelmed.

"Thanks to each of you. I'm so surprised. Thank you so much. Each of you has a special place in my heart. Philip, you continue to amaze me. Thank you." Several large tears dropped onto her blouse, still not realizing why this was about her.

Philip had agreed to escort Toni to the sorority's annual awards banquet. The honor was more special because her sorority mentor would be presenting the award to her.

After being presented, she thanked her mentor, the sorority and the guests. She started her speech with a distinction between giving and giving back.

"My generation consistently promises to give back when they finish degrees one, two, & three; once they are married, after they have given birth to 2.2 children; while driving that new BMW, Mercedes or Jaguar. We make these promises year after year after year. But, no one ever seems to hold us to these promises. The reason we are not made to keep these promises is because the people who are fulfilling the needs of our communities and the persons who need help in our communities are not holding us accountable. Now is the time for accountability. Would all of you who are forty and under please stand?

"Take note of those around you who are seated. They have paid their dues. Please take on their roles as your own. Allow them to mentor to you with their experiences and skills. Take the baton and let's get in the race. Combine those skills with your own and insure our progression.

"Would all of you who are ages 31 to 40 be seated? Those of you seated look at those standing. Would those of you standing, look at one another and look at me. I'm in the age group that's standing. The age group of thirty and under, you all are selfish. We have the Internet. We have banking on-line. We have entire conversations, locally and globally, with more than one person on a daily basis. Your mother probably doesn't know how to surf the Internet, nor do your older siblings. Use your knowledge to help expand the resources of those around you. Let's become accountable.

"I wrote this poem because we need clarification. I'd like to share it with you. "The Gift."

It will be a remarkable moment when you realize that this world is full of gifts such as

> Your breath,
>
> Your physical body,
>
> Your spirit,
>
> Your love,
>
> Your heart,
>
> Your talents,
>
> Your mind,
>
> Your ability,
>
> And most of all, your service to others

God sends blessings to those whom He can send blessings through
God gave His son – the most precious gift of all. Consider how warm you feel when you help someone with a bag or basket
Don't forget your emotions when you've helped a baby walk
Be mindful of the child and the smiles that come with his or her accomplishments. These gifts are priceless and unforgettable I remember when a dear person in my life read my favorite story to me at night. She read it over and over because I asked her to. I remember when she taught me how to ride my ride I remember that she gave me a flower when I won the spelling bee. But most of all, I remember she was there when I needed her. She held me tight, for she knew that I needed that hug. She must have needed one too because I let go first. She picked me up when my mom was ill and took me for ice cream and to the movies. Gifts are to be handled with care and love and kindness. They

each have their rewards. Remember that the gifts you share with someone may be the very thing they need to make it through the day until the next time. Don't take anyone for granted. Give of yourself. Give gifts.

"I'll close with the thought that we all have a responsibility to help those in need when they truly <u>need</u>. You owe because lots of people have impacted your life. When you were in need, how many times have you been turned away because that person from whom you requested help was busy? Did Grandmother say come back later after I get this degree or after I get this car? No, Grandmother put down her mop, her groceries, her cuptowel, and she looked into your eyes to search for your needs and met them on the spot. It's your turn to meet someone else's needs. Give gifts."

Philip stood and applauded loudly. The audience followed. The evening ended with dancing and a buffet. The glass plaque personalized with Toni's name was beautiful. An hour passed by before she realized how long they had been dancing. When they finally left and got into the truck, he pulled her close for a kiss. She didn't realize how long she had been in his embrace until the valet attendant tapped politely on the glass and gestured for him to move on.

Toni tried to sleep when she got home, but couldn't. She got up and decided to jot down her annual holiday letter. Postcards were already being made for the office.

Her draft went something like this:

"Hotep! Greetings! Praise be to my Lord and Savior from whom all blessings flow. This was the theme of my year: Blessings.

I will be thankful for each blessing this year. I will count them for you. (1) Health, strength; (2) Spirituality; (3) my business and my dynamic staff; (4) My new home; (5) My family and friends; (6) My community and its love; (7) My "Tabithas;" (8) The clinic and its growth; (9) A new, significant other; (10) A positive outlook on life.

The Lord was gracious and bestowed these items and brought me closer to many new people, as well as my family and friends. In addition, He sprinkled my year with vacations, gifts, and some of the best and wonderful experiences of all time. I have traveled to Atlanta, the Grand Caymans, Aspen, Miami, Aruba and made several trips to Kentucky.

The Clinic has expanded because of generous grants from several sources. The amount of services provided will increase. The number of people served will increase significantly.

The Church is growing spiritually. We completed payment of the church mortgage.

The credit union has been established and is being backed by a major bank in the city. Thus far there have been four million in deposits; much more than we expected. I have been elected as a trustee—the first of two women elected to the board.

The sorority awarded $25,000 in scholarships, four times the amount given in the past.

Last year was truly phenomenal. Praises to Him from whom all blessings flow.

Next year more blessings through faith. 2001's theme: Faith

I will have faith while accomplishing my goals. I implore you do the same. With any faith and trust, we will even accomplish some of those goals together.

My year 2001 goals are as following:

To improve lives by example;

To start an endowment fund for two scholarships; one for medical studies, and the other for economic or architectural studies; To start an investment group with concentration in African-American businesses and corporations that supports our community;

To start a book review circle;

To continue our current investments, both in time spent, and in money allocated, toward our present commitments; and

To support groups with physical and fiscal objectives and reinvest within our communities. We need to put our money and time in our communities.

To rebuild our homes, streets, etc. My desires for 2001 are as follows: To learn to sky dive; To hang glide regularly (I learned in Grand Cayman); To scuba dive regularly (I learned this in G. C. too); To visit the Smithsonian institute; To visit the Panama Canal; To visit the grave site of Malcolm and Betty

Shabazz; To go fresh water fishing with my great-grandfather; To learn to speak Spanish; To go to Africa; To complete my book; To learn to read and write Braille; To learn sign language; and To take a wine tasting class.

Most of my desires are academic; the rest are leisure. All of you are welcome to join me along the way. In the interim, pray for me and my goals, ambitions and wishes.

I once told someone that a wish is probably an unattainable desire.

With that in mind, I have a short wish list: To feed all hungry people; To remove abused children from their homes; To place all unwanted children in homes where they are wanted; To create a utopia where there are no murders, no crime, no loss, no sorrow and

Try to get along in this world. Competition is designed to build character. Loss was designed to break character. What are we warring over? We are not in competition for resources. We could easily share. The entity with the most resources generally wins. But we must ask ourselves if it will be at the peril of too many people? If we could share: you trade me oil and I trade you vegetables; no war is needed to complete such a simple transaction. But that would also support the theory that the government should have a bake sale to finance the weapons industry and finance wars, especially when our hungry citizens, especially those who served this country are in need.

1999's theme was love; from love blessings flow.

2000's theme is blessings; proof of blessings provide renewal of faith

2001's theme will be faith; faith leads to results

2002's theme will be grace; by grace we are saved

2003's theme will be humility; humility mirrors the image of Jesus.

We as a people need to have plans as we live the new millennium. So consider this a practice, or a dress rehearsal, because the first pitch is going to be thrown after the umpire says play ball. I want each of us to be ready.

As you travel and engage in other activities, please be prayerful and careful. My prayers are with you always.

Love and Happy Holidays,
Antoinette "Toni" M. Harden, M.D.

Toni handed Jackie her holiday letter draft on her way out the door to Kentucky.

"Jackie, can you email it to me so I can make corrections?"

"I'll do it. Here are your tickets and your gifts." Jackie held the door open for her. "I'm sorry your grandfather couldn't fly."

She and Jen had already sent her great-grandfather on the train, with a nurse Jackie had hired to care for him. She would meet them at the station. Toni's great-grandfather's doctor didn't release him to fly. In fact, she almost didn't let him go to Kentucky at all.

"I'm just glad he can go at all. What time does his train arrive?"

"A little after 3."

After her birthday, Toni had found an outside doctor for her great-grandfather. His treatment and care had become more aggressive. He was more active now. The new physician, Dr. Elise Cooper, moved him to a different facility. They formed a good relationship. Her great-grandfather told Toni he would move if that's what Dr. C wanted.

"Do you want to move with me? I have plenty of space." Toni questioned.

"No sweetie. I want to be where I am. I like your house, but I can only visit. I need to be with people my age."

His reply hurt somewhat. Yet, he was right. He needed to be in the care of a hospital staff. She couldn't do it, no doctor could do it full time. Dr. Elise put her mind at ease. The new facility looked great.

Philip's assistant dropped him at Toni's office so they could travel to the airport together. Again he tried to pay for the flight, but Toni had handled it directly with the travel agent.

Once they were settled on the flight, he kissed her on the forehead. Just then the flight attendant brought Toni a long-stem purple rose, a glass of champagne and a bowl of strawberries, accompanied by sugar and cream.

Chapter twelve

Philip was in awe of the Kentucky ranch house. Once they put their bags down, she gave the "grand nickel" tour. Philip thought that Toni had reorganized the house because the bathrooms resembled the ones in her home. In addition, he assumed that the fireplace and patios had been rebuilt. Later, he found that the only improvements were an additional oven added in the kitchen, an entire kitchen added in the cottage, along with some additional wiring. Now, he understood why she liked to come here. They had an hour before the train arrived. She noticed that Rita was preparing the downstairs bedroom.

"Did Elise call?"

"Yes, Dr. Elise said that he'll want a snack, maybe, and definitely a nap. We have all his medicine on stand-by just in case he runs out or loses it. She sent the instructions and faxed his normal diet. She had some oxygen sent too. Dr. Elise is quite thorough. She has a doctor on call, and has a room at the hospital on reserve. She requested that we not excite him too much. She must be your friend," Rita laughed as she continued to complete her preparations.

"Thanks, Rita."

Toni turned to Philip. He reached out and hugged her. They walked out to the stables holding hands. Jorge was outside watching the children skate while waiting on Toni to feed the horses. He immediately put her to work, while she asked all the right questions. She doesn't usually feed the cows; they're new. But today, she would do it all alone because Philip and Jorge were going to get the Christmas tree.

She introduced Philip to Cocoa, who licked his hand. She walked in the stable and immediately ran out to find Jorge. She was screaming by the time she reached the end of the barn.

"Was that your surprise? You could've told me. Oh my goodness, I'm so excited. With Mister?"

Philip stepped in and still didn't understand her outburst. Jorge was shaking his head. Toni was ecstatic. She ran to him.

"Cocoa is expecting a colt," Toni exclaimed to Philip. Then she turned to Jorge. "Has the vet seen her yet?"

"Yes, Dr. T. He knew you would be excited."

"I just wanted to make sure. Well, you guys go. The rental car just arrived. I'm leaving to get Papa in a few minutes." She looked at her watch. "Maybe I could use some help feeding after all," she laughed.

They returned about the same time with Papa and the tree. Papa decided to take a nap. Dr. Elise called as he was waking. They talked a while. He ate and retired rather early. He mentioned to Toni that he had forgotten how it felt to be in Kentucky.

Early the next morning, Toni and Philip rode Mister together. When they returned, breakfast was ready. They decorated the tree next. Toni had brought new ornaments this year. There was an ornament bearing everyone's name and the year. She also added bows.

The mid-day dinner was catered. The owner learned to make some of Rita's favorite dishes. Toni insisted that Rita be seated and served. Dinner was marvelous.

The children couldn't wait to skate. The weather in Kentucky was frigid; much colder than Toni had remembered. The lake was frozen over, so it provided a perfect opportunity for them to skate.

"Mr. Philip, aren't you skating?"

"I want to but I didn't bring skates." He hunched his shoulders. He kept his stance until the youngest one brought him a box.

"Open the box. It's for you." The youngest persisted until he consented.

"Toni! How did you know? You and your surprises." He simply chuckled. He knew Toni was as romantic as he. He put on the skates and met the children at the door. He didn't see Toni turn the corner, wearing her skates and ready to follow them to the ice.

She ran ahead to skate in front of them. She had natural, competitive talent. She still remembered the transition from a pirouette to an extended layout spin, and still performed it flawlessly. She had given up skating because it held no future for her. She had competed enough to pay for college and some of medical school.

Philip was quite the athlete although he wasn't a proficient skater. It was tradition at the ranch to turn on the lights before the first person went to bed. Rita made tea and hot chocolate and they roasted marshmallows. The children usually opened one of the gifts Toni brought. One of the presents was for their birthdays. On their actual birthdays, she sent some money and a savings bond.

Papa was extremely sentimental. He nearly cried when the lights came on. He was up slightly past his bedtime. When he told her he loved her, she cried quietly. She tucked her great-grandfather into bed. Toni retired shortly after Philip.

Chapter thirteen

"Hey!" Tabitha greeted Toni with immense excitement. "I'm so glad you're here."

"Me, too, Tabitha." Toni hugged her tightly. They had both been looking forward to this dinner for months.

"The caterer said the food would be served in about forty minutes."

"Okay. Philip is unloading the tree. Help me get the lights. We can start decorating now."

"Okay." Tabitha followed her to the truck.

Toni and Tabitha stayed back to talk.

"How's school?"

"It's good. I like recess and reading. I like it."

"The teacher treats you okay?"

"Yeah, she tries to look after me. The other day she sent some clothes home for mom, but she waited until they picked me up after school. She doesn't say a whole lot but I see her looking with that look on her face."

"What look?"

"Like she's worried. Kinda like that face you made when you first met me."

"So you need anything?"

"No, not really. I just like going to school. Thanks. My little sister and brother are in school now, too." Tabitha stole a look at Toni to see her expression.

"That's great, Tabitha," Toni said, silently thanking God.

Tabitha was doing well in school now. Her teacher emails Toni and has become equally involved in her progress. Toni had to convince Tabitha's parents to let her get an education. When her dad finally agreed, he nearly made Toni regret her persistence. Now she knew that she had done the right thing. Nothing could replace the memory of Tabitha's expression when Toni took her shopping for school clothes and supplies. Toni also arranged for her father to get more work.

Overall, the family improved. Tabitha seemed much happier. Her mom also found work and was taking an English class at the community college. Her dad got a small business grant from Toni's bank to improve his business and hired employees, including one of his sons and other family members. He was doing better than ever.

Dinner was excellent. The caterer did a wonderful job as usual. Tabitha told Toni it would be a good idea to serve the meal like family-style instead of having the plates already full or making a buffet line. Toni agreed. She didn't want to put the family on the defensive. They really liked the food; and the dessert was delicious. The caterers left after dessert was placed on the table. Tabitha's father's eyes grew misty, and a tear fell when he saw the angel light the top. He walked over to Toni, who was standing with Tabitha, gave her a hug and kissed her on the forehead. He hoisted Tabitha onto his back and they stood at the door as Toni and Philip drove away. Tabitha signed "I love you" behind her dad's head, something she recently learned in school.

Toni was exhausted after her full day. Tomorrow was full, too. The community service center was having the Christmas social. They served dinner at the center to those who need a meal and some extra spirit. Each doctor donated new ornaments to decorate the tree. They also collected toys for children who might not receive anything from their families. The children really enjoy it. The evening's treat was a visit from Santa Claus. The female doctors rotated turns. Since it was Toni's turn, Carolyn's assistant dropped off the suit at Toni's office.

"Would you like to spend the night?" Toni winked at Philip. They had not been alone in several days, and needed him to run his fingers through her hair and massage her temples. They just needed to relax.

"Yes, I would like that. Would you like me to draw you a bath? I would really like to give you a massage." Philip placed his hands on her shoulders.

She stood speechless while he gently massaged.

"You lead a very intense life, you know that?" Philip asked. "You deserve the blessings that come your way." He turned her to him and held her face in his hands, then snuggled her in his chest. He rocked her gently until he felt her exhale. He felt her body relax and he tightened his embrace.

Toni melted in his arms. He felt so good. His hands were on the back of her hair. The uncertainty, the tension, and the exhaustion faded under his firm, yet, loving touch. She had tried to raise her head to say yes to the bath, but she couldn't. He felt her moving, so he guided her up the stairs to her room and laid her down. He returned with the massage oil after he started her bath water.

He kneaded the knots from her slim shoulders and back, and Toni sighed beneath his touch. He massaged her muscles until they were no longer tense. She moaned as he passed over her shoulder blades to her lower back. After a few more movements, she was asleep. He tucked her in and took the bath that he had drawn for her. He wanted to be Toni's everything. He could be the man that she desired, needed, and deserved. He had fallen so easily.

Chapter Fourteen

Usually they ate at a restaurant, but since she had just moved, she decided to have this year's party at home. Jen selected a seafood theme. She said, "Toni has had enough traditional Christmas dinners in the last three weeks to last a lifetime." She served crawfish and shrimp etoufée, with fried seafood and other goodies. Jackie passed the pictures from the community center around after they had lunch. Kiki couldn't help but laugh at Toni as Mrs. Santa Claus. Kiki could see that she was having a good time and the children were enjoying her too.

They decorated her tree after the laughter over Mrs. Claus passed. Philip had moved the ornaments out of storage for her earlier that week. He also bought her tree for her. They were supposed to go together but rounds lasted longer than anticipated, so he picked a perfect fir that fit well in her living area without her. They had a smaller version in the office that the children enjoyed decorating. There was an ornament with each child's name, as well as special trinkets for Toni and the staff.

They had hot chocolate after they turned on the lights. The lights caused Toni's crystal antique ornament collection to sparkle. Toni brought out a box of gifts and envelopes for them. The gift exchange was always interesting. They were supposed to buy for the person whose name they pulled for 'Secret Santa,' but that was not always the case.

Jen surprised Kiki with wine glasses and a bottle of wine. Jackie was exuberant when she saw the compact discs, and a replacement set of headphones from Daphne.

Jen opened the white box holding a photo album made of lace and ribbons she and Jackie had seen a month ago at a bridal show. Jen nearly knocked the table down between them. Daphne waved the box around to confirm that Toni had bought her some pots. She had just moved and knew that Toni must have overheard that she didn't have any.

Kiki giggled when Toni opened the box with the dog food, dog book, squeaky ball, and water/food dish with "Bubbles" hand-painted on the side. There was also some medicine and a brush included in the box.

Toni wondered why Jackie had disappeared. When she returned, she was carrying a small, black puppy in her arms. Jackie lowered her to the floor, and she was attached to a purple leash. The dog walked around and pawed each of them, as if she knew them, and then she finally hopped into Toni's lap.

Jackie offered, "She's been looking at a picture of you for two days. She almost blew our cover yesterday. One of the kids came in the storage closet behind me and saw her and she screamed. She and I had to have a long private talk. I had to promise a bunch of stuff so that she wouldn't tell."

Kiki returned with the rest of her things. "This is our group gift. We adopted her from the Society for Prevention of Cruelty to Animals. We talked to Philip and this was all he could come up with."

Her staff had even involved Philip in their purchase.

"Cameron picked her up and kept her the first day."

"We picked it out," stated Jackie and Daphne.

"This year we were at a loss—we had no idea." Jen explained.

Toni picked her up and Bubbles kissed Toni in the face. Toni thought she was adorable. "Thank you guys. I love her. I suppose she stays this small, or relatively so?" Toni asked while Bubbles frolicked in the used wrap.

"Yes, this is it. She's housebroken. She has a tub lined with paper. She gets in and does her business and hops out, and then she comes and gets you to show you. She will go outside, but when it's cold she doesn't finish. We talked to Philip and he says he'll talk to you about adding on a 'doggie door' to the garage. We talked to Darius and he thought that we were crazy to do this. We didn't think of that until it was too late." Daphne seemed a little worried that Toni would be mad. Toni was actually excited.

"I'll keep her next week while you're gone," Jen volunteered.

"Okay. I know each year I promise not to do anything extra but you all mean so much to me that I have to do a little extra. The wrapped gifts are from me personally and the envelopes are office bonuses. You all have done phenomenally. I love each of you. You're a good team. I do appreciate each of you and what you bring to the office. So here you are."

Jen received a gift certificates from Victoria's Secret, and Dillard's, where she was registered, and some money with a note to talk to Toni when Toni returned from the holidays. Kiki revealed a briefcase. Daphne opened a box of dishes and a gift certificate to Crate & Barrel with a list of "must-haves." Jackie received a framed print of a ballerina that Jackie's boyfriend disclosed that she wanted. They all got a gift certificate to Bath & Body Works because they could never get enough bath stuff.

They ended that evening singing Christmas carols and sipping champagne. They were off for the next two weeks. Toni was leaving on Saturday for Vail. She wished them all a happy holiday.

Toni still had to pack. She had a little shopping to do. She called her answering service to be sure they knew how to reach her.

"Precious, how did your party go? I wanted to stop by." Philip's voice soothed her.

"You cannot be in cahoots with my staff. How long did you know about this dog?" She knew he remembered that she wanted a dog.

"Sweetie, they asked me because they hadn't heard anything. They said that neither Jelly nor Darius would give them any leads. Of course, I wouldn't give them my ideas. So we came up with the puppy. It took three visits to finally come to a happy medium of which puppy to get. I hope you like her. I knew it had to be cute and it couldn't be big.

"Anyway I called to see if you needed anything. Are you still going into the office tomorrow?"

"No, I'm not going to the office tomorrow. I have some shopping to do. I have to drop off the puppy and the family's Christmas gifts. Jelly and Darius will be here at some point. They decided to sleep here so they wouldn't have to drive early Saturday. I would like you to come too.

"They didn't say what was going to happen with their companions, but I extended the invitation. What's your agenda like?" Toni laid back in her favorite chair and Bubbles was immediately in her lap.

"I want to cook breakfast for you. We won't be alone for several days and I would like to spend some time with you."

"I would enjoy that. Do you plan to come over tonight?"

"That was my plan."

"Bring your things for Vail as well, if you want."

"See ya in a few."

"Okay."

Toni hung up the phone and exhaled. She wanted a man who was not afraid to be a man, someone who needed little reassurance for security. Maybe Philip was the one. He was so giving. He understood her need for intimacy without invading her space. He had the skills of a great companion. Mostly, Philip understood her vow of celibacy until marriage. She loved Philip.

The phone brought her out of her thoughts.

"Your beeper must be in your purse. I have been paging you. I forgot your office party was tonight. I finally decided to call you at home. Anyway, what time do you expect me tomorrow? Also, I'm bringing the fixings for enchiladas and tacos. Is that okay or did you have something else in mind?" Jelly always spoke so swiftly.

"That's fine. Is your friend staying the evening?"

"Yes, I'm bringing him."

"Do you know about Julia?"

"I don't think she's coming. Darius didn't mention her when we spoke."

"Enchiladas and tacos are fine. The doorbell is ringing. I've got to go. It's Philip. I'll see you around three."

"Bye, Toni, see you tomorrow."

Chapter fifteen

Toni woke up on Christmas day to three inches of snow. Perfect skiing weather. She was on her way to the window when she realized that Philip was still asleep.

She was still in awe of Philip. He had been everything she had needed, hoped for and desired. These last few months had been phenomenal. There were nights out to dinner, to the ballet, the opera, and the many gifts he had given her. Their long talks meant the most. Their trips had been wonderful.

Thanksgiving in Kentucky was more romantic than she could've ever imagined. She was fascinated by Philip. She thought maybe she was even ready to introduce commitment to the equation. Although she didn't date or see anyone else, when she had had lunch with Raymond and another friend, she always thought of Philip during those outings.

A knock on the door brought Toni back to reality. She opened the door, and a silver tray rolled passed her. The waiter smiled slightly when he saw her face.

"Madam, could you please be seated at the table?"

"Okay, but if this is breakfast, I need to wake Philip. Let me go get him."

"Ma'am, I have detailed instructions. Please be seated." He draped a napkin in her lap as she sat down. He noticed her nervousness as she looked around for her companion. He continued following his instructions. He poured two glasses of champagne, coffee for Philip, and tea for Toni. He placed the strawberries and a waffle at her place setting. He placed blueberry pancakes with scrambled eggs at the other place setting. He placed the other condiments on the table, along with a bouquet of purple roses and a large box.

"Good morning, Beautiful. Sleep well?" He was wearing purple silk pajamas. She wondered when he changed because that's not what he wore when she said goodnight as they parted to their rooms.

"Yes, actually I did. And you?"

He bent to kiss her gently on the nose and lips. "Too well. Merry Christmas." He could tell she was surprised.

They prayed together. They ate quietly except for the laughter that erupted when their eyes met. She noticed more snowfall and knew that meant that skiing would be limited. She wanted to play in it though. When they finished, he presented her with the box, "I have something for you."

She looked at it with a raised brow. It was very well wrapped. It just occurred to her that she hadn't seen this box while they traveled. She opened the box. She pulled out a black, Mark Cross handbag and wallet, which contained a few hundred dollar bills, a Mark Cross watch, and at the bottom of the box there were two plane tickets to Australia.

She gasped. Her breath was gone. She looked up at Philip. He was smiling because he knew that she wasn't expecting that. She went to hug him.

"Thank you." Her eyes still wide with surprise.

"My pleasure," Philip leaned back in his chair satisfied with the fact that he had surprised her and she had no answer. Finally he was able to do for her without her giving him something too.

He wanted to love her and she allowed him to love her and to spoil her. He didn't want to rush her. She had been receptive to his attempts to fulfill her needs. She had catered to his needs as well. He was very content with her. But, he wanted the next steps as well: her commitment, her heart, her soul and her hand in marriage. He wanted it all. He loved Toni.

She was so sexy to him. She was as excited as a child about the snow. She brought him over to the sofa and they lay in each other's arms and watched the snowfall together until lunch. He rubbed her hair until she fell asleep.

Each couple seemed to have energy that was passed on to the next couple. Each woman had received one gift in private, so they shared that first. Julia, Darius' friend, received a gold initial pendant with a necklace. Jelly received a leather jacket from

Martin. Toni shared her purse, watch and Australia tickets. It was not over though. Among the most remarkable gifts though was Darius's gift from Julia, a Movado watch. Martin gave Jelly a claim check for a car stereo system. Toni couldn't even match Philip's gift with her offering of a Cole Haan wallet, leather jacket, Cole Haan shoes and a claim check for a hand-tailored suit.

Philip resembled Santa. He was wearing a red sweater and black turtleneck with black jeans and black boots. Surely she could spend the rest of her life with this incredibly handsome man. He brought a box in and placed it in front of her. She looked at the box and then at him. She lifted the lid and moved back the tissue paper to unveil a full-length, mink coat. He lifted the coat out of the box and helped her put it on. She was so moved. She would've never guessed he would give her a gift of such magnitude, especially since he had just given her the tickets to Australia. A pin drop could've been heard it was so quiet.

Toni reached for Philip to hug him. He caressed her back and her hair. He felt her let her guard down. She started to feel comfortable, comforted, relaxed and safe. They parted from their embrace.

"Thank you just doesn't seem to be enough. I need some more words."

"Darling, thank you is enough, besides you render us speechless often. Actually, there's no need to thank me. I did what is in my heart. I love you."

"I love you, too."

♦♦♦♦♦

Once they parted, Philip approached Darius, "Darius, I wanted to talk to you because I want to ask Toni to marry me and I wanted to know how she'll respond."

"Man, are you kidding? You didn't ask me about the coat," he jests, "Man, that's great. I know that she cares about you and she loves you. She talks about you all the time. I think that you should go for it. You are both very good for one another. And you understand her intensity. Although, she hasn't said anything directly, nor to me personally, I think that it would be a good move." Darius sat down at the bar and ordered two Crown and sevens. He sent three glasses of wine upstairs. Just then Philip saw Martin and motioned for him to come over.

"Thanks, Darius. I had a good indication, but I wasn't sure. How has the trip been so far for you, Martin?"

"Fine man. That was one hell of a coat. That's a husband move."

"I'm trying to be, man. That woman makes me fall in love with her on a different level each day."

"I guess the wine didn't get upstairs fast enough. Here they come." Darius shook his head in disbelief.

"Yoohoo, lover boy! It's time to play." Jelly wrapped her arms around Martin's neck and kissed him loudly in his ear.

Philip turned around to greet Toni with a hug. Julia had one arm on Darius' shoulder.

"Where's mine?" Jelly pouted.

"Yours is on the way upstairs to see you, but you are here so your drink is looking for you. So sit still and be patient. You'll have a drink in a second." Darius motioned for the bartender. They had sent a bottle upstairs so the bartender poured three glasses of wine for the ladies.

Their concierge came by and told them that the Carolers were in the lobby. Also that dinner would be in the Great Room in one hour. They got their drinks and moved to the lobby by the fireplace.

Toni noticed, "The snow is falling again." Philip found a spot for them on the bear rug. After a half an hour, the ladies excused themselves to freshen up.

"Toni, how long have you known Philip?" Julia seemed a little shy asking this question.

"About one and a half years, we've been dating for about three months, and it's been such an intense courtship. Why do you ask?" Toni replied.

"How long have you two known Darius?"

Jelly responded, "We've known him about ten years. They went to college together. We met through Toni. Why do you ask?" Jelly wondered where this was going.

"I just wondered about the depth of your relationship with Philip because of your mannerisms and his. You two seem in love. I'd like to experience that passion, that intensity," Julia said expectantly.

"Darius is capable; give him some time. Do what makes him respond passionately, intimately. Remember, you can only be intimate with one person at a time. You cannot share your time. You will lose focus. Philip and I have spent some real time together. In the past six weeks, we have been on three trips, and a bunch of intimate day and night excursions, none of which were physical. Most importantly, we talk to each other about each other and about ourselves. We are moving somewhat fast, but we are interested in the same things and are flexible to try new things. We have invested time in each other. He did get out of hand today with the coat but I can't tell him that because he did what he wanted to do for me. So, that's that." Toni continued to fluff her hair.

"What you can do is have patience. You are doing well from an outsider's perspective. If you want more, you need to invest more. You need to ask for more. Darius isn't crazy," Jelly stated as a matter of fact.

They headed back to the Great Room where the guys were waiting on them. The food was interesting. It had a South American flair; reminded her of Americas. Toni hadn't been impressed with hotel food in a long time. They returned to Darius's suite with champagne, and strawberries.

They sang more carols and prepared to ski the next day. They had been there for two days and they had only been to the slopes once.

Chapter sixteen

New Year's Eve was exciting. Philip lived in a semblance of an adobe in the historical Third Ward-museum district. The day had been warm, but it cooled off somewhat that evening, so he had dinner catered on the patio. A band played turning the second half of dinner into a party. Several couples dropped by as they finished dessert. They danced about ninety minutes until the limo came to take them to the jazz concert featuring Toni's favorites Kirk Whalum, and Fourplay.

Although last minute, they had great seats. The concert opened with the comedian, Billy D, whose popularity exceeded expectations. The concert was phenomenal. She and Philip actually danced in the aisle. The concert lasted for what seemed like hours. When they finally returned to Philip's, it was 2 AM. They had forgotten that the New Year had started.

"I would like to propose a toast. To great friends." Darius turned to Jelly and Toni, "To the next year filled with mystery, wonder and love." He looked at each couple with his glass raised and then looked down into Julia's eyes. He bent to kiss her and Philip followed his lead.

Philip disappeared for a moment. When he returned, he raised his glass to speak, "To the joy and wonder of this past year and to the splendor of this one to come. To our daily blessings and to a phenomenal and gracious woman." His eyes glazed over as he looked beyond Toni's surface into the depths of her soul.

Then Toni raised her glass, "To all of you and to what each of you mean to me individually and collectively. I look forward to a year of prosperity of the heart, mind, soul, and of our collective efforts." She took a dramatic pause and was about to complete her thought when Philip interjected.

"And to the rest of lives together as friends, lovers and soul mates." Philip turned to Toni and placed a ring on her hand. "Will you be my bride for the rest of our lives?" Philip kneeled in front of Toni and waited on her response.

She lifted him from the floor. They embraced tightly for several moments. Toni felt tears slide down her face, then she felt a tear drop on her shoulder. His heart beat softly in her ear. She pulled back slowly to see his face. She kissed him lightly on the lips. She spoke slowly, "Yes, Philip, I will marry you. Yes, I will spend the rest of my life with you. Yes, I will be you friend, lover and soul mate for eternity."

Philip gazed in her eyes and they engaged in a long, passionate kiss. They would've continued except their company demanded their attention.

Jelly cleared her throat. "Excuse me, you two. I believe that congratulations are in order." She hugged Toni, then Philip. She held Toni's petite hand in hers to admire the three-carat, brilliant cut diamond mounted in platinum.

"Philip, this is gorgeous," Toni dabbed her tears. The proposal matched her dream almost exactly.

"Man, I keep wondering when you could peak, but you just keep making her speechless. Congrats, man." Martin shook Philip's hand.

"Man, look I'm tired of you showing us up," Darius joked. "Take care of her man. Make her your best friend." They did the hug-shake thing that men do.

Darius turned to Toni, "Love him with all of your heart. Take care of what you asked for." He kissed her on the frontal lobe and said goodbye.

Congratulations were said all around.

"Will you stay with me this evening? I want to stare at you until the dawn. To grow accustomed to waking to your beauty, to your love."

"I love you." Toni spoke so softly it was as if just her lips were moving and no sound came out.

"I love you, too." He pulled her to his chest where she rested her head.

Chapter seventeen

"I'm on my way. I'll meet you in the ER at St. Lukes." Toni was tired of this hospital. She needs to own a wing she was here so often. It was 3:00 pm, so she wouldn't be returning to the office. She would just have to finish on Monday.

She looked down at her left hand and remembered that she hadn't told Philip. She hopped in the BMW just as the phone rang.

"Hello. This is Toni."

"Baby, where are you? Do you want me to have someone to come pick you up? I just heard."

"Thank you but I'll be at the hospital in a few minutes. Dr. Elise didn't seem alarmed."

Philip feared that Dr. Elise hadn't told Toni the whole story. He knew that he had to have someone meet her in ER. Toni was going to lose it.

"Okay, baby. I'll be here when you get here. I'm attending in ER today. Be careful." He knew full well that she only had to travel a few blocks, yet he still worried about her reaction when she arrived at the hospital. He dialed his assistant, Cameron, to have him come to the hospital. He called Jackie for the same purpose.

The ER was crazy, but Toni floated through ER as if nothing was wrong. She found Dr. Elise who brought Toni up to speed. Dr. Elise didn't seem concerned about his current condition, which led Toni to believe that her great-grandfather would be okay. Toni spent some time with him. Jackie already sent balloons and a plant. Philip was seething by the time he found Toni.

"Baby, what's wrong?" She touched his arm in an effort to calm him.

"I'll be fine. I was just worried. Go back in and I'll see you a little later." She couldn't recall seeing him like this. Cameron missed Toni when she came into the hospital, so Philip worried about her whereabouts.

She showed Papa the ring and talked to him about Philip. She talked about Christmas and asked where he wanted to go next. She babbled on and on while he drifted in and out of consciousness. She was just about to leave when he opened his eyes and spoke.

"Baby, I love you. Thank you for all that you do. I'm glad that you are going to marry Philip. I wish I could be there. I miss your grandmother." He motioned to hug and kiss her and he whispered good night.

"Good night, Papa." She pulled the door behind her.

It was late and Philip's shift was over so he waited in the hallway until she came out.

"Hey you!" She was concerned to see his solemn look.

"How is he?" Philip stood.

"Well, Dr. Elise should probably think about releasing him on Monday. I didn't read his chart but I'm sure that he'll be fine. I'm coming in the morning to feed him. He held my hand tonight. He is still strong. He said some special things. I must show you a picture of my great-grandmother. She was so beautiful. Are you coming with me? Have you eaten?" She paused just so he could answer.

"Yes, I'll stay for a little while. Maybe we could stop and pick up something to eat." Philip knew for certain that she did not know why her great-grandfather was in the hospital. Dr. Elise did not tell her and he knew why she didn't, but he was so afraid.

"Let's just order a pizza. I have movies at my house. We could fall asleep in front of the TV. There's also some wine chilling in the refrigerator." Toni gave her smile. Fear crept back into his heart.

"Hello, Dr. Harden speaking." Toni spoke in her most raspy voice.

"Dr. Harden, we need you here right away. It's your great-grandfather."

The next thing she heard was a dial tone then the car engine. She and Philip arrived at the hospital last. Elise, Darius, Jelly, and Daphne were already there. They live closer. Toni rushed to the door of the hospital room but she knew that it wasn't good. She remembered the talk they had.

"Baby, he died just a few minutes ago. He suffered very little. I'm sorry." Darius pulled her into his arms and placed her head on his chest. He felt her body jerk with sobs. Suddenly he felt her pull away. She turned on her heels and within a split second she entered his room.

The nurses were clearing the equipment from his room. Toni dismissed them. She preserved the warmth in his hand in hers. Her tears kept flowing. His eyelids were closed. He looked peaceful. She wished she had been there. She cupped his hands until she felt the coolness seep through his skin. She turned to see Philip standing at the door in near darkness. She kissed Papa on the forehead and the hand and said a prayer in her heart.

Philip maneuvered her to the waiting area. She managed to stop crying just long enough to send Daphne home. "Thanks Daphne. I'll see you Monday."

Elise went home after they signed the death certificate.

Jelly spoke softly, "The funeral home will be here in thirty minutes."

"I'll handle it," Darius assured. Toni wandered to his window and waved bye once more.

Toni sang at the services; the same song she sung when she would comb his hair, "His Eye is on the Sparrow." The services were emotional, yet beautiful. The mourners ate dinner at the community center. She was the picture of composure until the limo ride to her home with Philip.

"I can't believe he's gone. I loved him so. I miss him already." The tears streamed down her face. She had lost her very best friend. After all, he was her fishing companion. He coordinated many of Galveston's fish frys. He taught her to drive the riding lawn mower, much to her mother's dismay, of course. He showed her how to catch her fishing bait, crawfish. She learned later that they tasted good if boiled. He witnessed her lake accident while she attracted minnows for his bait. He was there when she received her ten-speed bike. He taught her to bake a cake, make a hamburger, scale and filet a fish and cut a chicken. He has been there for her in her times of need as well as her triumphs. He was definitely her best friend. He kept her secrets. She would miss him dearly.

"I know," Philip responded.

Philip put her head on his shoulder. Toni's tears softened. She had been taken by storm, but she knew that this was best. His 83 year old body was tired. She knew that her great-grandparents would be together which made her smile. Philip perceived her calming. He rubbed her hair. He finally felt her exhale. When they arrived at her home, she crawled into bed and was asleep in about 15 minutes. Philip sat in the chair in the corner and watched her sleep.

Chapter eighteen

Toni reflected on Philip's love and support. She would've never expected so much compassion and sympathy. She thought that surely she lost all credibility of needing someone. To her surprise, in a short period of time, he had become the best friend and soul mate for whom she had prayed. He amazed her.

The wedding date had not been decided. She pulled out her Franklin to jot some possible dates. She needed about 4 months to plan so that put her at May, May 14th looked good. It was far enough before Memorial Day, but it was only a few days after Mother's Day, actually a week exactly.

"I have looked at dates for the ceremony. May 14th looks good. How does that sound to you?" Silently hoping that he agreed.

"Baby, that is fine. How are you doing?" It was Sunday morning, and she wasn't dressed for church. He was certain that she was still in the bed and this concerned him. He needed to be there. He wasn't sure of exactly what she needed but he knew that she would have normally been at church already.

"I'm struggling. I really miss him. I saw next week's schedule. I won't have a chance to breathe." She paused at the thought that Philip had been so attentive. "Thank you for all of your love and support. I look forward to us spending the rest of our lives together."

Philip always responded slowly and thoughtfully. When he asked Toni to marry him, he was sure of what that decision entailed. He was pleased with their progress and the attitude that she exhibited. However, he was sensitive to the fact that she exhibited a strong exterior while protecting a very sensitive interior. This interior being caring, loving, sensitive, motivated and most of all, giving. "You are welcome. You know that I would do anything for you. I am glad that the rest of our lives are important to you. I want you to be happy more than I want my own goals."

"I'm going to get ready for church. Are you coming with me?"

"Sure. What time will you be ready? Have you eaten?" Philip was actually walking out of the door at that moment. He committed his life to Christ at an early age. He wasn't as active as he wanted because of his surgical career and travel. This didn't impact his spiritual growth. However, he knew that knowing God's order for marriage was important. His commitment to Christ held importance. His spirituality would make the difference in their marriage. Philip recognized that his spirituality and knowledge of the Lord set the tone in their relationship. He usually attended church in the neighborhood but today he considered becoming a member of Toni's church.

"I'll be ready in about an hour. No, I haven't eaten," Toni said.

"I'll be there in about 15 minutes." They hung up the phone.

He picked up a white rose on his way. He envisioned her blushing when he handed it to her. He felt her lips on his. He felt her small but strong arms around his body and on his back. He smiled at thoughts of her dimples deepening because he brushed his nose against hers. He heard her giggle as clearly as if she was standing right there.

"Congratulations! Toni, I'm so proud of you. You really deserve it. When did you find out?" Philip pulled her into his arms. He knew that she had been nominated because he had voted for the AAD presidency, but he had not read when the results would be announced.

"The chair of the election committee called today. I'm not sure if she called the other officers. As a matter of fact, that may be my job. I didn't even ask. I'll also have to meet with the outgoing president to discuss the transition. He wasn't supposed to call either, but we made an appointment to meet. They are both very excited. Philip, I need you involved so you need to contemplate your role, other than the fiancé of the president." She smiled knowing that he would remain active, but remembered that he would be on the ballot for his fraternity as chapter president.

"Come on Toni. We're late. We said that we would meet them at 6." He opened her door and closed it gently behind her.

He pulled the car into the valet just behind Darius. Toni didn't realize that Jelly was behind them until they all hopped out.

"Morris, party of six." Philip approached the hostess stand with confidence.

"Dr. Morris, please follow me. Is upstairs okay?" She kept walking as if Philip had agreed. They were seated in the Wine Room of Ruggles Grill.

Jelly heard Philip order a bottle of champagne. "What's that about?" Jelly spoke barely above a whisper. Toni ignored her to talk to Darius. Philip heard her though. He winked at Toni signaling that he heard her.

"This has turned into a celebratory moment for Toni, and not at a better time. You all are looking at the new president of the Houston Chapter of the American Association of Doctors."

"Congratulations, Toni." They all said how proud they were of her.

Over dinner, the conversation kept on the upswing. "Toni, when are you going to start planning for the wedding?" Julia asked.

"Actually I have started planning. A noon church wedding, of course. Four attendants on each side. Jelly and I are going dress shopping next week. I've considered having one made, but I don't think I have that kind of time. I met with the seamstress and we selected material for their suits. I've actually gotten their measurements too. Kimberly found the shoes and already sent them to me. It's in May. So I have 3 ½ months." She reached over and kissed Philip. She laughed at Jelly who was mocking her by kissing Martin.

Philip added by saying, "I have actually reserved the tuxedos and had my measurements taken. And actually two of the groomsmen have had their measurements taken as well. Only Darius and my best friend have to go. Last week, we met with my frat brother who is the coordinator and florist. Next week, we meet with the pastor. The coordinator will handle most of the arrangements for Toni. The reception will be at the new Museum of African American History and Art." He reached over to hug her. She stole a kiss and giggled a bit.

"You have been really busy. It sounds like you're almost done. I don't know how you find the time. Let me know if you need anything," Julia offered.

"It didn't take long. Once we set the date, plans fell in place. And remember, we have a coordinator. The invitations will be printed in two weeks. Also, the honeymoon has to be arranged. Everything should be complete by the last week in April. There are three showers scheduled, one is coed from the AAD," Toni continued.

"Darling, the honeymoon is done," Philip asserted.

"I see I stand corrected," Toni blushed.

"Not to change the subject, Philip, tell me more about the museum." Martin interjected.

"I am one of 15 founders and trustees. We financed the building ourselves. The contents are being sponsored by various entities. The first traveling exhibit is "Africa and its Splendor." The exhibits stay three to four months. We have several membership levels. We will have some free memberships that we raffle off at the opening gala, which is next month. Toni is coordinating the opening. She's been involved from the inception. She initially declined the Board position, but now they have my help to encourage her. We weren't working on it together before because we didn't know that the other was involved until I talked to her before I presented her award late last year. She knows that we need her. She is an incredible asset for the museum. Anyway, I'm excited about the museum. It's the first of its kind in the region." What Philip neglected to mention was that they wanted Toni to be the chair of the board. The trustees met recently and they asked him to ask her. He advised that they get her on the board and then elect her to serve as chair. He was excited but he wouldn't push too hard.

"Well Philip, let us know so that we can become members. I was so excited when I heard about it. I didn't know that I was so close." Martin handed Philip his card.

Once outside, they all said congratulations again, then said goodbye. Toni confirmed their shopping trip with Jelly. Jelly also reminded Toni to go pick up the things that she ordered last week. Toni didn't know it, but Jelly bought her the shoes that she said that she liked. She would find out when she picked up her other things. It wasn't often that Jelly was able to surprise Toni. They hugged. Toni promised to call.

Chapter nineteen

"All rise. Judge Jennifer Blalock presiding."

"Thank you. Please be seated. Good morning, Counsel. I have reviewed the will in question for the deceased Mr. Joseph Robinson. Counsel, are you prepared to begin?" Acknowledging their nods, the Judge proceeded. "We will hear the will. Then if there are any questions, complaints, plans for appeal, then we will address those at the end of the reading. After I hear those additional discussions, I will rule. Anything further, I will advise. Then we adjourn. We will be done in approximately one hour. Madame Court Reporter if you please, read the last will and testament of the late Mr. Joseph Robinson."

The court reporter began to read. The document started with the standard items of mental stability, willing everything to his wife except in her death. She continued to read his wishes where he gives property to his adopted daughter, grandson, and some varied family members. She read the date and the signatures of himself, witnesses, and his attorney, whose son was here in his place today. Toni did the math and this document was written nearly 17 years ago. She would've been 11 at the time. The estate was estimated at about $175,000. The court reporter kept reading because there was an addendum.

The addendum read as follows: "This is to replace the previous will and testament document. I leave all of my worldly possessions to my great granddaughter, Ms. Antoinette M. Harden, also known as Toni. All before mentioned items and any extraneous articles are to be transferred to Toni at the time of my passing." Signed by Mr. Joseph Robinson, three witnesses, and attorney; dated September 5, 1998.

Her attorney offered his handkerchief as did Philip and Darius. She took Darius' as it was already in her lap. The other members of the family exploded in disbelief.

"Ladies and gentlemen if another outburst occurs, I will hold those responsible in contempt and will dismiss you all. Now please take your seats so that we can proceed. Counsel for the State, do you have any issues?"

"No, your Honor. All of his debts have been satisfied. Counsel is here simply to confirm. The State rests." She returned to her seat.

"And counsel, you represent Ms. Harden?"

"Yes, your honor, I do."

"Do you have any additional information?"

"Your honor, I have evidence of care giver status of Ms. Harden. Receipts, letters and other documentation relating to his care over the last few years are available at your request. His attorney is here to present any other documentation needed. We are only here in the event of an appeal or in the event that it was needed."

Papa's attorney then spoke, "I visited with Mr. Robinson upon his request and he was of sound mind and spirit when he did both documents. He states on the tape where we recorded the statements as well as a handwritten letter as to why he made changes, to his will and what outcome he expected. He said that he entrusted me and my firm to insure that his wishes were followed to the letter." He approached the bench with certified copies of the documents and then returned to his seat.

The Judge took a minute to examine the documents for authenticity. She had the contents of his safety deposit box, so she compared to handwritings and concluded that the court would uphold the wishes of the deceased. Now only she, the State attorney, and Papa's attorney knew what the letter said.

"First of all, the documents are authentic. The handwritings match. The wishes of the deceased will be upheld. The compelling portion of the case is his letter in support of his own will. I'm going to read a portion of that letter. But before I do that, I am ordering all possessions be released to Ms. Antoinette Harden. Several assets have been frozen. The State will lift those restrictions. Ms. Harden, those assets are now yours. I am truly sorry about your loss and hope that you can resume your normal life soon. His letter reads:

"I changed my will not because she loved me, cared for me, supported me and visited me daily; but because she was my best friend. She has been the only friend that I have had since my wife died some

years ago. It was good to have someone to tell stories to and to have someone to listen to me. She would sneak my favorite stuff into the home. She wanted to move me out totally but I didn't want to go. She respected my wishes. I love her and want her to have all the things that were once mine. She doesn't even need them but after this soul is gone, my things are all she'll have to remember me, so they will belong to her..."

By the time the Judge was finished reading, everyone in the courtroom was close to tears if not already crying. The Judge dismissed the session but asked to see Toni in her chambers. Toni made an appointment with the two attorneys for an afternoon lunch. Before she went to chambers, the State's attorney handed her a package and her business card and asked her to be in touch.

"Dr. Harden, please come in and have a seat." The Judge hung her robe on her door and sat behind her desk. "I asked to speak to you because this has been a special probate case. Your disposition is commendable. Families can get really ugly. I'm glad that this was handled so well. What made your great-grandfather create a new will with all of the formalities and the letter and all?" The Judge crossed her legs at the ankles.

"Judge, please call me Toni. I was only informed of the letter after he passed. So I only have what you have. I knew that there had been a change to his will but I didn't know that this was the result. I suppose his attorney suggested it. We never talked about this. We never talked about death." Toni moved a tendril behind her ear.

"Well again I'm proud of you and I will make sure that nothing is reversed. I'm really sorry about your loss."

"Thank you, Judge. Have a good day." Toni walked out and sighed. Families are truly ugly sometimes. She had enough of family dissension to last her quite sometime.

Philip, Darius and Andre waited for her in the lobby of the court building.

She was more concerned with title transfers for property than a possible appeal. Andre promised to research the tax status of each property and get back to her. She was most concerned about the personal effects, which had been left for her, particularly his military flag and war medals.

She glanced at the package that the other attorney had given her. She still didn't know what was in it. At first thought, she considered giving it to Andre and have him report on the contents. But she was curious so, she decided to look inside later.

♦ ♦ ♦ ♦ ♦

Once at home, Toni sunk into her favorite leather chair. She scanned some medical material, then she remembered the envelope, large and brown and heavy. She spread its contents on the floor. She flipped through some photos before she started with her great-grandmother's will and memoirs.

Toni remembered the ring that her great-grandmother left her. It bore ten brilliant amethyst stones in a white gold setting. Papa presented the ring to her on their twentieth wedding anniversary. Granny wore it on special occasions. It was dainty while quite a conversation piece. It was one of Toni's favorite pieces of jewelry. The ring was of the type which was never duplicated.

She also found her great-grandmother's journal. Toni thumbed through several pages until she ran across the story of one of the fishing trips that Toni and Toni's great-grandfather took. As Toni read, she could hear Granny's voice.

> *"I never shall forget. Papa had practiced with her so that she could throw out her line. She was strong as I remember. One day after a long practice, she decided to ask. She asked however while they were outside. Toni knew that I was scared of her fishing. Joseph wasn't strong enough to save her if she fell in the lake. I told her father to go even though she would want to be alone with her grandfather. They talked for hours about everything. Well as she was asking, he came in the house and she reluctantly followed. She knew that was the end of her privacy. She also feared that I would resist her desires. Well, later I shared my fears with him privately. He assured me that they would be careful. He said that she had worked hard and deserved a chance. Her dad had picked up her weather boots from the other house. She was even ready to catch her own bait, of which earlier she had been afraid. They had practiced catching bait one day after a hard rain. He told me that they would be going tomorrow. The crawfish would be out in the morning and they would catch them before breakfast and leave afterwards.*
>
> *She woke up so excited; I worried. She dressed before breakfast, rushed her chores and was ready to go before Joe had completed*

dressing. She waited patiently in the front room as if the most important visitor in the world was coming. When they finally left, she was beaming as bright as the sun. Her dimples had definitely deepened.

When they returned, she ran up the steps with fish on a string in one hand and a big plastic bag in the other. She held out her capture for me to see. She yipped in excitement over her 3 big mouth freshwater bass. The other bag, she lay at my feet and walked to the kitchen more somber than excited.

As it turns out, she was trying to catch her Papa some minnows because she looked in the bucket and there weren't many left. He was fishing for trout. She decided to help. She had the burlap net in the water and when she pulled back to catch the minnows, she got stuck in the mud and lost her footing. She fell in that mud. The pants that she had been wearing were in that bag. They went to her grandmother's house so that she could change clothes. Her dad arrived just as she was falling. He said that it didn't seem like she was upset that she fell. When Papa realized that she had fallen, he dropped his reel trying to get to her. The loss of the fish and minnows bothered her more than actually messing up her clothes which was a surprise to everyone. She was always making sure that she was clean and neat.

The coolness of the tears arrested her attention so she stopped reading. She missed both of them so much. Her whole concept of family was diminishing before her eyes and there was nothing that she could do about it. She patted her face, then flipped though the rest of the documents when she ran across her grandmother's, her dad's mother's, birth certificate. What she read was quite shocking. Toni's great-grandfather was not her grandmother's real father. He did later adopt her, though. The adoption documentation followed. Then it got deeper. She read the facts and events in her family history, which she had never known.

Toni's intense focus caused her to nearly miss the phone ringing.

"Hello?"

"Hello, sweetheart. What are you doing?" Philip asked.

"Actually I'm reading that package that the States' attorney gave me. I'm finding out some interesting things, like my dad's mom was not my great-grandfather's child. I found out that I have a half sister, and that at 14, she gave her baby up for adoption. My great-grandmother's memoirs are in here as well. It has been great reading her most intimate thoughts.

"Anyway, what are you doing?" Toni had actually started feeling better. His voice had perked her up.

"I realize that tomorrow is a workday and filled with obligations but I wondered if I could take you to dinner and dancing?" Philip smiled because he knew that she was surprised. He just wanted her to relax. He planned a couple more surprises for later. "Could you be ready in 45 minutes?"

"Philip, I was so comfortable. Where?"

"Don't worry about that. Just put some clothes on."

"Okay, Philip, but we can't stay out too late. I need to be at the gym at 6 in the morning and the office by 8. I do staff evaluations this week at the hospital."

"Okay, I'll be there shortly. Bye." He had to take her mind off this latest news. She had enough to worry about considering the estate, the "new" family history, work, her social obligations and most importantly, him and their marriage in a few short months.

"Jelly, the other night Philip took me to Brennan's and then to Maxie and Jake's. We danced and danced. I had such a good time. I really needed that. I relaxed. I let all of that stress wash off of me." Toni met Jelly at the Galleria to search for dresses.

"I forgot to tell you the things that I found out. My father has another daughter, older of course, who gave up a baby at 14 for adoption. My great-grandmother's first child was stillborn. My father was actually a twin but the other brother died in a swimming accident when he was 8. I cried nearly the entire way through my great-grandmother's journal. Ooh Jelly, there were even some entries in my great-grandfather's handwriting. Her notes later revealed that he wrote those entries because she was in so much pain she couldn't write. She even talked about my birth. That part was extremely moving. Her imagery was fabulous.

"Anyway, the envelope also had keys and deeds to properties, vehicles, and such. Bankcards were included but the account was closed through the State. They issued a check to me for the funds in each account. He had saved the last of his military benefits and social security payments. It included beneficiary statements where now I'll get those payments. I've inherited two homes in Houston, one in Galveston, two riding lawn mowers, and several hundred tools. Andre said the estate closure is complete. I'm so glad."

Toni and Jelly browsed through more wedding dresses. This was the third dress shop and Jelly was about to give up. Their suits would be ready next week. She had less than three months and hadn't found "the one." She and Jelly both flipped through hundreds of magazine pages. Not one dress stimulated her interest from several hundred dresses. Toni was looking for something contemporary and unique, while embodying ever so slightly the traditional element.

When Toni described the characteristics, Jelly knew that they were in trouble. There was no way that a store bought dress would do all of that.

They were seated at Café Annie's when Jelly broke the bad news. "Toni, please get your dress made. It would be easier that way. You are not going to find something that says 'something' and meets all your criteria with a dress from a store. Besides you don't even have the twelve weeks that it takes to order a dress.

"I don't mind looking but when I know there's no hope because of your tastes, you have to face the truth. Let's go see the tailor and get this underway. You need the dress within the next six weeks anyway. You do intend on taking a bridal portrait don't you? If we call now, I'm sure we could go today." Jelly proceeded to call the tailor. They were in the Galleria and the shop was in the Village. "We can get there in no time."

"Okay Jelly, I'll go. Let me sketch something real quick." She sketched a gorgeous gown. She had imagined this dress for years. It took but a minute for her to design her dream dress. They finished their meal and went to the designer.

Toni was amazed that the tailor had some designs already. She took out her sketch and they made a new sketch with the best components of the designs. Toni was pleased with the final design.

Jelly laughed. She knew she was right. She smiled and winked when they left the tailor.

Chapter twenty

"Dr. Morris! Dr. Morris! We've got a patient on her way. Blacked-out. Low blood pressure. Her neighbor said that she had been suffering from severe headaches. She's about sixty years old. She's on life flight. ETA twelve minutes. We have OR 3 being prepared now. Dr. Miller said that she would assist. Your staff is on standby. By the way, your office called. Do you want me to call them back for you? Cameron sounded nervous." Allison was the assistant to the chief of ER. They were rushing from his rounds in the east wing to OR in the north one. She radioed ahead that they were on the way.

"The chief said that your assistant is on his way." They reached the OR and Allison parted ways with him, heading back to the ER.

The fact that Cameron was coming bewildered him. "Kate, are you ready?" Philip stood by Dr. Miller as they scrubbed.

"Haven't done this in a while. What's the story?" Dr. Miller paused with her hands in the air while waiting to be gloved.

"I'm not exactly sure. I don't have the medical history. I have no chart. I was just called away from rounds. It looks like our patient is in the ER. Let's move."

The next few moments were intense and extremely precious. This woman's life rested in Philip's hands. They wheeled her in and immediately prepped her for emergency surgery.

Philip glanced up casually. The chief of staff usually watched in emergency surgery. Today, he had an entire audience. In addition to the chief of staff, the chiefs of ER and

OR, his assistant, and a pleasant surprise: Toni. When he caught her eye, she waved nervously. His assistant, Cameron, kept checking his watch.

"Let's start with possible blockage to the brain. We may have a tumor. Let's check the passages to the brain."

"When is someone going to tell him that she's his mother?" Cameron spoke sternly, being cautious that OR intercom was off.

"He doesn't know?" Toni squirmed more. She knew that sooner or later he would find out. These were not pleasant circumstances.

She could tell that someone was reading to him. She flipped the switch so that she could hear. The nurse was amidst medical history. He looked curious. The OR nurses all averted their eyes from his. He knew that there was something they were keeping from him. Just as he had that thought, his physician's assistant walked into the OR, he looked up and saw Toni hugging his sister, and the nurse reading the chart to whom he had long ago stopped listening said Mrs. Morris.

Philip stopped cold.

"Dr. Morris, BP is dropping. Dr. Miller, vitals are unstable."

"Philip, what is it?" Kate pressured him to begin moving again.

Allison radioed for the surgeon on standby. She was in the OR within seconds.

"She's my mother." Philip tried to continue working on his mother's fragile body but his own heart skipped a beat. How could they think that he could do this? He couldn't stop. She had to make it. She simply had to make it. He kept working. He realized that Dr. Branch was standing at his shoulder.

"Philip let me. They just found out. They really had no idea. Your assistant had been trying to call to tell you, but when he didn't reach you, he assumed you knew and just came over. He called Toni while he was on his way. They were the only two who knew." She took the instruments from his hands. He moved away slowly. He looked up. Toni had disappeared. He walked to the scrub room where the nurse cleaned him up.

Toni reached the door just in time. She heard that long, shrilling beep. She saw the tears roll down his face. The nurse was nearly done. Toni reached for him while hoping for a heartbeat, but the beep persisted. She heard Dr. Miller call for clear. She watched Philip agonize. She steered him out to the waiting area. She watched the tears roll down his strained face. She could not imagine his pain. She looked up and saw Kate, Cameron, and Dr. Branch. She knew they had lost her.

Kate sat down on his other side. "You're a brave man. She had two blocked arteries. There was no way anything could have been different. Please know that we've done everything that we could. It hurt me to lose her, too."

His tears kept rolling. Cameron stood opposite them and just stared. Philip's P.A. walked up and sat down. She too, looked on in agony. Toni was still in shock.

"Philip?" She stood in front of him while his head was down and his elbows rested on his knees with his hands together. He opened his eyes to see his sister's feet. He stood to hug her. His touch and her tears were simultaneous. He tightened his embrace. This was the closest that they had been in years. Her husband walked up and took her by the arm.

Toni turned Philip to her. They held one another. When Philip finally pulled away, his eyes glazed over. Allison brought his keys and pager to Toni. She asked Cameron to call her office and explain that she would be there shortly. Toni dropped Philip at home then headed to her office. Cameron said he would stay. His sister pulled up as Toni was leaving.

When Toni returned, she finished two appointments. She totally forgot that her new systems would be installed today. They had scheduled some tutoring that she would simply have to miss. She needed to return to Philip.

His sister was asleep when Toni arrived. Her husband had gone to get their son. Cameron was on the phone. Philip was sitting on the porch of his bedroom staring out at the yard. She startled him when she opened the doors.

"Thank you, Toni."

She kneeled in front of him and rubbed his leg ever so gently. He put his hand in her hair and returned her attention. He felt so loved. He pulled her up and walked her inside. She sat him in the chair opposite the television. They held hands. He kept so quiet that he startled her when he spoke.

"I need you to do some things for me, please. My sister and I need you right now. Mom's neighbor called me a little bit ago. I'll need to go there today. I'm ready but I'd like you to drive, please. I'll drop Cameron by the hospital to get my car. Then I need you to help with the arrangements for mother's funeral services. Toni, it's just me and my sister. We can't do this. We weren't ready. I know that this is a lot, especially since you've just been through this. Please help me." His words got caught in his throat.

"Yes, Baby I will. Don't worry." Toni went downstairs to speak to Cameron.

♦ ♦ ♦ ♦ ♦

Philip shuffled around for an old box. He remembered his mother putting important papers in this one box. He found her keys and her bankbooks in her purse, so he figured the rest should be found in the box. He poured over the box when he found it. He pulled out just what he needed: the medical insurance card, life insurance policy, and her will. Philip's dad died shortly after he was born, in the Persian Gulf war on medical duty. Though he died years before, Philip and his family had only probated his father's will a year ago. Philip made his mother very comfortable once he was able. The house was in his name. He paid her expenses. She got social security but she used it for pocket change. He had wanted her to live with him, but she insisted on living alone. So their compromise was for her to move closer to him. She had moved from Lufkin, Texas, where he grew up. She knew that he loved her and she wanted to live with him, but he wasn't married and she feared that her presence would deter overnight guests, which is not what she wanted.

He kept shuffling through the box. He found their birth certificates, his father's death certificate, and some other documents and their passports. He also came across her diary. He pushed the box aside and closed his eyes, and laid his head back on the leather headrest.

♦ ♦ ♦ ♦ ♦

Toni's mind started clicking with what to do first. She would use the same funeral home that she had before. She wondered what he wanted to do with the house and her belongings. She feared what emotional state they'll reach once they cleaned her house.

She would approach these topics slowly. She had yet to decide what to do with the property that she inherited. She had already stored all of Papa's personal effects. Jackie and already placed the ad and sold those pieces. The Star of Hope picked up the pieces that she decided to donate. The other pieces would be moved next week. That left the three houses. At least one had to be sold. Anyway, she understood the issues that he faced.

She stopped at a little bistro where she relaxes from time to time. She knew that it would make Philip feel better. They would eat and have relaxing conversation.

"My mother will miss our wedding. She spoke of you as a queen. She sincerely wanted to get to know you better. She was in awe of you and wanted me to be happy. She felt that you would enhance my happiness. I so wanted that you would be friends, but I know that she's better now. She often ignored her health. My father inspired me to be a doctor. Without his pale skin, he may have never been a doctor in the Marines. I didn't aspire to be an officer though, I decided to do it the long way.

"When I graduated from medical school, Mom sat on the stage with me holding a picture of my father in her lap. I talked of my inspiring parents; my dad's influence for my love of medicine and the need to stay and protect my mother and sister, my mother's influence to be scholarly, and take advantage of all opportunities. She cried even more when the entire audience applauded loudly when I introduced her. That was one of the best moments of her life.

"Toni, she was struggling this morning. I wasn't able to help her. I could do nothing more than I did even though she was my mother. The fact that I couldn't help her hurt more than losing her altogether. Toni, what's frightening is that I felt her give up, her life. She stopped fighting. That's why I have to remain strong because she was so strong for us." A single tear fell on his shirt.

Toni sang "Wind Beneath My Wings" at the memorial services. The audience had been in tears for the entire service. Mrs. Morris was highly decorated as a member of Zeta Phi Beta Sorority Inc., an Eastern Star, a Link, and a Top Lady of Distinction. She had been very busy. It finally occurred to Toni why Philip didn't have a problem with Toni's social involvement. He was always encouraging her to be involved and was proud of her activities.

The services were longer because she was a practicing Catholic when she died. Philip eulogized his mom so well. His words flowed like a river. Toni was moved to tears.

"When did you stop practicing Catholicism?" Toni asked when they were finally alone and on the way to his home.

"My mother converted to Catholicism when we were in college. I've always been a Baptist. We were rather shocked when she did it. We think that one of her girlfriends persuaded her to convert."

"Thank you for everything. Don't you feel the dejá-vu?"

"You certainly know. I think my love reached new unbelievable heights during that time."

"I've fallen in love with you everyday for a while now. I'm ready to wake next to you everyday. I'm ready to love you under one roof. I'm so ready to be your husband. See, I'm already married to you. Our hearts and souls joined long ago. I'm just waiting on the date." He leaned over and kissed her. She blushed.

"Don't forget the fraternity's gala next week. The museum grand opening is in three weeks. Let me know what you need if anything," Philip heaved a heavy sigh, realizing that no amount of small talk would take the pain away.

"Sweetie, please. Those galas should be the farthest thing from your mind."

Chapter twenty-one

"Jackie, updates, please?"

Jackie proudly announced, "You are receiving a tax refund. It isn't large, but it is a refund. The new systems are working well. There have been no complaints. The rest of the office improvements have been completed."

Toni was impressed. They had been on autopilot for at least two weeks, if not three. Toni wanted to own the building, as a separate entity for primarily African American owned businesses to be together. This would allow for two things: one of which would be recycling money in the community, and the second, African American businesses have the opportunity to be in a "high rent" district without the actual high rent.

At the close of the meeting, Kiki brought in a box and Daphne followed with a floral arrangement. "He is definitely consistent." Kiki remarked about her latest gift packages, knowing that Philip was the sender.

"Put them on the conference table. If these are from Philip, then that means that he didn't get much done today." The card made her smile.

The box was something different. There was no card outside. As she opened the box slowly, there was a large card on top of the purple tissue. Her heart thumped harder. She glanced over the card. She focused on his words: "Our love is beyond tangible definition. I love you always. Love, Philip." She put the card down and looked into the eyes of Kiki, Jackie, and Daphne, who were just as curious as she. She pushed the tissue back. She found a pair of evening shoes. Next, there was the jewelry box. There were even nylons.

Then there was another layer of tissue. She pushed that layer back more slowly than the first. Her eyes grew large with surprise. She eased a garment out of the box and held it to her. The black silk gown was gorgeous. The back scooped deeply bearing a split in the front on the left. One look at the designer's label, "Couture by J.R." shocked her completely, as this was the same tailor for her bridal gown. The last card in the box read: "Wear this to the Museum's Opening. I hope you like it. P.M."

Everything matched perfectly. His thoughtfulness overwhelmed her. His gift solved half her problem. She still needed to find something to wear for the fraternity gala.

"Thank you for my packages today." Toni bubbled with excitement when he answered the phone.

"What are you talking about? I know nothing about any packages. Your other man must've sent something. What did he send?" Philip knew that she didn't like when he played like that. This time was a little different.

"He sent me a beautiful dress, some matching jewelry, hose and shoes. He included gift certificates for my hair and nails and feet. He arranged for a limo to pick me up. He also sent a picture of his platinum card." She laughed. She knew that the tables had turned and he wasn't accustomed to that. She didn't really favor his humor in that manner, but today it was a little funny.

"Oh, he did. It seems that I have some competition. I have some catching up to do. I have a plan." Philip laughed. "Did you like the dress?"

"I do! I love it. You are such a giving person, such a loving person. I love you for that. You possess pure love, and care and passion. That's why I love you."

"I love you, too, Toni."

"Are you ready for Friday's gala? What else do you have to do?" Toni questioned.

"I'm ready. Cameron picked up my tuxedo today. Everything else is in order. The gala is completely sold out. Interestingly enough, all of the money has been collected too. Door sales will be out of control. This will be the most successful one yet. I was worried about that when the president appointed me as chair last year. It was not well organized in years past. By the way, I will need to be there early, so there will be a limo picking you up. I want to dine with you before because I won't be able to at the gala. Do you think that's possible?"

"Don't worry about that. We can eat afterwards. You need to be available if there are any last minute problems. I really could drive myself to the gala. Do you need a limo to pick me up?"

"I don't want you to drive yourself home though. Please let me do that for you. At the door, you will be seated at my table. Some museum people will be there whom you'll recognize. Some doctors will be there that you know. By the way, I could get seats for Jelly and Darius and their guests if they would like."

"No, I don't think they are coming. I got museum gala tickets for them. I'm looking forward to it. We put the final touches on the planning this week. I still have to buy a dress. We have some wedding preparation to do, too. Have you given any thought to groomsmen gifts? I may get the bridesmaids gifts while I'm out. But my veil is my real priority."

"I gave their gifts some thought. I was going to talk to you about that."

"What are your plans for this evening? Have you eaten? I was going to Café Express to grab a salad. I could bring you something if you would like." Toni picked up her keys and her handbag.

"I'll meet you there. I don't want you to go by yourself. See you in a few."

Chapter twenty-two

If this event was any indication of what was expected at the museum's gala, they would take the city by storm. The gowns were stunning. The tuxedos were fresh. And the food was absolutely fabulous. The scholarship program was timely. They danced and danced. Toni even saw some women without shoes. Finally, they inducted their new leadership. Unlike Toni's sorority, their new officers learned of their new position at this gala. Toni knew several of the new officers, but she was most excited that Philip had been elected president. She was even more surprised when he introduced her in his acceptance speech.

 He was so handsome. When she watched him from her seat, she squirmed with anticipation. He had her heart. She felt him in her soul. Soulmates. She was proud of him. She never wondered if he had worries or fears, she couldn't imagine that he had any. She had her own fears and maybe he thought that she didn't have any. She displayed a strong, emotional peace. Most presumed that she has it together. She gave off the impression that nothing disturbs her equilibrium. She wished that she didn't give off that aura sometimes, but it was unavoidable. He gave the same strong, impenetrable front. She knew his true gentle nature, his calming spirit, his intense passion, matching hers. She was so intrigued by Philip. His total element engulfed her. She was in love. There was no doubt about it.

♦♦♦♦♦

Toni had been nervous since they called a week ago. Philip would be here in moments and she still had a half dozen things to do. She couldn't get her earrings on and Jelly promised to help. She thought a glass of wine would help calm her, but the results were slow. She needed Jelly. "Where was she?" she thought to herself. Toni took the earrings downstairs with her. She had almost completed her makeup, but her lipstick was downstairs, too. She nearly dropped her glass on the stairs when the doorbell rang. She tried to calm down but her deep breaths didn't help.

Jelly moved past her. "Okay, sit. Earrings. Lipstick. Necklace. Powder. Drink. Dab. Breathe. Calm down Toni. You will do fine. The gala is going to be phenomenal."

"I had to give an interview yesterday. I didn't realize that there was a press release announcing this. I don't know why not. Of course, I didn't see it until Wednesday. I'm glad I've had all day to prepare." She eased to the entryway mirror. "I'm still a little nervous."

"You'll be fine." Jelly heard a door. "That must be Martin." Jelly went to the door. Toni retrieved her wineglass from the bar.

Jelly returned with a floral arrangement. "This man knows no time of day." Toni knew not to even ask. Philip had struck again. Martin arrived shortly before Philip. She anticipated driving her car because the dress was not conducive to stepping up into his truck or seated low in the Benz. When he arrived, she decided that he thought of it, too. There was a limo waiting outside to transport them to the gala. Philip doesn't miss many details.

"Please gather and salute as we are led in the national Negro anthem, "Lift Every Voice and Sing" by a member of the Museum's Board of Directors, Dr. Antoinette M. Harden."

Toni approached the microphone. She sang solo beautifully until she reached the second verse. Her voice led the audience through the second verse and then they repeated the chorus. It was so harmonious, that they almost didn't want to stop.

A member of the Trustee Board returned to the podium. "Please join me in welcoming your mistress of ceremonies this evening. She is a fantastic pediatrician, the president of the American Association of Doctors-Houston chapter, and a board member of the museum. I'm most proud to announce that she has been elected the chair of the Board of Directors. Your songstress, Dr. Antoinette M. Harden." The thunderous applause was deafening.

"Thank you. Thank you. Thank you to my fellow board members. Thank you to the Board of Trustees for the confidence that you have in me.

"Welcome to the first African American Museum of History and Art in this region." She paused and absorbed her audience. Her apprehension instantly faded.

"You are a part of life changing history: 'The museum will change your life.' The museum is a national phenomenon. We have made significant landmarks with its opening. The trustees have provided the sole funding for the museum. The underwriter list has grown without solicitation. This is the culmination of the Kwanzaa principle "Ujoma," economic development and independence. This evening following our short program, we will have various activities. Please take advantage of this phenomenal event.

"The program will proceed as follows. We will be greeted by the chairman of the Board of Trustees, followed by remarks from John Hope Franklin and Gordon Parks, then I will return to close the program and direct you to all of the activities for this evening.

"The chairman of the Board of Trustees is a nationally recognized neurological surgeon and specialist at the Texas Medical Center. He has been the recipient of the Randolph Award, the most prestigious accolade a doctor can receive from the AAD. He is a native Texan, hailing from Lufkin. He is an active member of his fraternity's local chapter as President. He is a warm man with a passion for our people and our community's survival. Please welcome Dr. Philip Morris."

"This is by far one of the most moving and historical events you may ever experience. I welcome you. This endeavor has been one well worth each challenge. The special guests dined with local high school seniors who were the city's top performers in school in both academics and extracurricular activities. Mentoring is just one of the programs that the museum has started."

After a few more comments, Philip passed the program onto Dr. Franklin.

The depth of the program intoxicated the audience. Their ovations when both Dr. Franklin and Mr. Parks took their seats was breathtaking.

Toni returned to the podium, "there are eight areas of the museum where activities are taking place. The two book signings in progress, Nikki Giovanni, Susan Taylor, and Iyanla Vanzant in one area with Colin Powell, Gordon Parks, John Hope Franklin, and Kweisi Mfume in another area. Michael D. Cheers will lead the art tour. Several "Songs of My People" pieces are now permanent property of the museum. Dexter King will lead the history tour. Mrs. King was unable to make it, but sent her well wishes. Several children's authors will read their books in the children's reading room. The library and gift shop are open so you may browse.

"Finally, the membership contest winner will be announced in about an hour, so be sure to enter. Most importantly, have a great evening. There is one group I need to introduce—the team wearing red jackets. They are ready to answer any questions or clarify anything.

"Thank you and I bid you a great evening."

She hurried upstairs. Her coordination efforts brought the first joint board dinner to fruition. They hadn't all met at once. Both she and Philip had some announcements to make. In addition, the board members reviewed their biographies because they would be published next week.

Toward the end of the meal, Philip thanked everyone, especially Toni. Toni and Philip excused themselves to visit the mentor dinner. They made several stops around the museum before approaching the door to bid their guests farewell. The board members, trustees, and special guests started to trickle down. The photographer took some last minute photos, including several group shots. Toni hugged each of them as they left.

Philip and Toni were nearly the last to leave. They sent the staff home moments earlier. The director, Gina Lightfoot, walked out with them. "Gina, thank you. We couldn't do any of this without you."

Gina responded, "We issued four hundred new paid memberships. We have an additional two hundred and sixty memberships committed. The attendance was approximately seven hundred." When her car arrived she simply waved goodnight.

They rode home in a comfortable silence, her head resting on his shoulder. He beamed because of their successful evening. Toni was divinely gorgeous. She was the humble and elegantly meek woman who he continues to fall in love with.

The opening proved more successful than planned. As Toni reviewed the videotape, she recalled some of the finest historical memories and some of the most prominent figures of this time. The videographer managed to capture priceless moments, some of which Toni viewed for the first time. Toni couldn't believe the public's response to the museum's opening festivities, which made the front page of the newspapers in Houston, Dallas, San Antonio, Austin and Galveston. There was also coverage in the Atlanta,

Chicago, New York and Cincinnati media and in USA Today. The National Black Press featured several stories and photos. A couple of the articles highlighted sections of the remarks made by Dr. Franklin and Mr. Parks.

Philip received several calls about additional sponsorships. Banks, and the oil and gas industries requested meetings with Philip and the financial officers. Although Toni was excited about the funding, Philip appeared unmoved. "When we approached these same industries, they were non-responsive. Now that the media has covered it and it has been nationally commended, they want to sponsor. I'm not in any hurry to respond to that. We have the community's support now. I'm wondering do we really need their contributions."

"They realized that they needed to support the museum. You should at least consider hearing their proposal," Toni suggested.

"Maybe."

This was the first time they didn't agree on an issue, which surprised her. While she understood his point, she still wanted him to give them an audience.

They had exceeded all expectations to this point. She knew that this venture would be long lasting. They had overcome all the public's doubt. The national impact had been phenomenal. With the gala's success, Toni became responsible for all other social events held at the museum either for the museum and other organizations.

Several board members called with similar sentiments of their pleasure for the event. A couple reminded her that she would have to coordinate the meeting dinners as well as all other functions requiring food and guests. She chuckled. Event coordinating was her hobby, although she did it well, she would never do it full time.

Chapter twenty-three

"Turn your head a little to the left, Toni. Now have a seat. Okay, look down. Less smile." The camera kept on clicking. Toni moved slowly. "Look into the mirror, Toni. All smiles. Turn to face me. Step out a smidgen. Hold it. Turn to the side. Hold your head down. Okay, now walk to the prayer bench, kneel. Hands together. Head down. Walk to the brown wall. Left hand over right in front of your dress. Shoulders back. Head centered. Okay, head down, over shoulder looking at end of dress. Look at me. Look at your hands. Look at the bouquet. Sit on the stool. Put the Bible in your lap. Put your feet on the shoebox. Sit back. Relax. Hands on Bible, left over right. Look at me. Look down at hands. Hold spine in palm of right hand. Keep left hand on the side of Bible. Read. Okay. We're done here." The photographer gathered his equipment to head to the museum.

The limo waited downstairs to take Toni and Jelly to the museum. The wedding coordinator would meet them there.

"The pictures are going to be gorgeous. He's good, where'd you find him?" Jelly questioned.

"He photographed the fraternity's and museum's gala. Remember I told you that Philip arranged this. So it's no telling what else may happen. In the museum, I'll be walking around in the art gallery. He will also want to do the fountain and the globe. I'll need to wear the veil and I forgot to ask Terry to come and put it on. Do you think we can manage. I tried it with her once."

Jelly touched up Toni's makeup and hair. "Yes, we can do your veil. You're a little nervous?"

Toni put her gloves in her lap, along with her handkerchief. "A little."

Even though it was a quiet Sunday afternoon at the museum, Toni still managed to attract the attention of the guests. She walked through the galleries posing next to various pieces.

A little girl walked up and touched her dress and the photographer shot Toni looking over her shoulder at the little girl. What Toni didn't know was that the photographer also got a picture of the little girl picking up the train of the dress. Then she stopped and walked closer to Toni and touched her at the back of the knee. But when Toni picked her up and started to walk, she was intrigued. The best one perhaps had to be the one where the little girl had her finger on her lip while admiring a watercolor piece. Then of course, there were the ones where she and Toni are gazing at one another, face to face.

"How old are you?" Toni inquired of the little girl.

The little girl held up her two fingers to her cheek indicating that she was two years old.

"What's your name?"

She looked toward her father and turned back to Toni and babbled something that sounded like Hope. Her father mouthed it to confirm.

"I've never seen this," Hope's father confided in Jelly.

They followed the photographer carefully. Jelly positioned her veil on her head securely. When Jelly turned her back, Hope raised the veil and kissed Toni.

Her dad reached for her, "Come. Let's go. Wave to the lady." She waved good-bye to Toni.

Toni pulled back her veil to wave and blew her a kiss. "It was nice to meet you. Thank you." Hope blew a kiss back. Toni hoped that Jelly had gotten her address and phone number. She remembered that the photographer had one of her cards and sent him to give it to the father.

♦ ♦ ♦ ♦ ♦

"Hello Tim. Thank you for coming."

"No problem, Toni. How are you today?"

"Fine. I just finished the bridal shoot."

"Oh great. I was going to ask about that."

"I have prepared the last of the details for you. I'm ready to hear your ideas and whatever I need to know."

Tim opened his portfolio, "I have here the timeline for the day."

Toni handed over her lists, "Jelly will be making some last minute calls to remind people of their duties so whatever you need, we'd like to know now."

"Well that's fine but I could do that. I have everything I need to do all of that for you." Tim continued to review the details.

They were seated in the atrium. It was 'Staff Sunday,' so when Toni had lunch catered for the staff, she included the three of them.

They finalized several details regarding the wedding. Toni's excitement escalated when he described her flowers. Toni shared the fact that Philip's mother had passed and his favorite aunt would be lighting the unity candle. Philip nearly died when Toni asked him about it. His aunt had graciously accepted. She knew that Philip wasn't handling his mother's absence well.

They walked through the museum and discussed the layout of the reception including the food service, bar, the tables and all the decorations. Once they completed the walk through, he reviewed the final ceremony details over the lunch.

When she and Philip talked last about the plans, one of the bridesmaids hadn't paid for her dress, the gloves were going to be late, the printer couldn't find one of the ribbons needed for the programs so that they matched the invitations, and a couple of shower invitations had been returned. He offered to assist with the printer and the returned invitations. He knew that she had to handle the rest. She seemed grateful for the assistance. She knew that he was stretching by offering. Not because he wouldn't but because she gave the impression that she didn't need any help. This of course wasn't the case. She had never been clear of how much he wanted to do or how involved he wanted to be. But as usual he came to her aid selflessly.

Toni had chosen to keep the wedding party small. The program read "friends" instead of the traditional "bridesmaids" and "groomsmen." Instead of bride, everything referred to the traditional bride as "Her," consequently Philip was referred to as "Him." She ousted every wedding tradition, except for the unity candle, the church ceremony, and Christian music.

Chapter twenty-four

"Mrs. Harden, hello. This is Philip. I'm calling to take you to lunch. I want to talk to you about Toni and the wedding. Can I pick you up at about eleven?"

"Sure, Philip that's fine." She heaved a heavy sigh. She usually avoided conversations with anyone Toni dated.

Philip hung up the phone, "Cameron, she said yes. So, I've got to go. I've got to pick up some things first. Don't forget that cookie bouquet for Toni."

"What do you want the card to say?"

"'Surprise, sweetheart. Thinking of you.' I just wanted her to smile. The planning for the wedding is stressful but she would never admit it. Thanks, Cameron."

On the way to Mrs. Harden's, he mapped out his conversation. First, he decided that they would start with stuff about her childhood. He didn't know much. He was somewhat curious about why she and her father weren't speaking. He didn't find this out until she announced that she would be walking alone. He was somewhat stunned, but he let it go for the moment. He knew that there had been some tension at her great-grandparents' funerals but the details escaped him. He hoped that her mother could clear up some details for him.

He wanted to know why she wasn't more involved with the plans. Mrs. Harden hadn't been involved at all. They didn't even shop for their dresses together. "I wonder if she even knows what Toni's dress looks like," he thought. He was concerned about their relationship. He wanted Toni to be happy but he knew that the relations between her and her mother had been strained for a while. He hoped that he could better understand the situation or at least make her mother aware of the issues Toni shared with him. He knew that this had to be the most dangerous way to achieve the answers he wanted. He discovered that Toni was not very vocal when it comes to her feelings. Her mother may not even know the issues that Toni was dealing with.

He remembered one occasion when Toni left the office at mid-day.

"Toni, please."

"Dr. Morris, she's not here."

"Something happen? What's wrong?"

"It was kind of sudden really. I beeped to let her know that she had two calls holding and a few messages. I didn't get an answer. When I looked up, she was walking out of the office without saying a word. We went on business as usual. Then her mother called and insisted that she had just spoken to Toni insinuating that Toni was still there. I spent ten minutes assuring Mrs. Harden that Toni had left the office for the day. I remembered Mrs. Harden saying that Toni was unappreciative and some other negative comments."

Jackie didn't take a breath, "I hate their distant relationship." Then she abruptly stopped.

"Thank you, Jackie. If she should call, please have her call me."

Since then, he has wanted to get to the bottom of this and help them become closer. He couldn't imagine what the issue could be. Toni was a mother's dream. A successful, independent doctor, who was invested in the community. Most of Toni's generation had boomeranged; back home that is. She was not a regular daughter. She deserved all that her mother has.

Midway through lunch, Mrs. Harden looked up from her salad with glassy eyes. She spoke slowly, almost laboring.

"Philip, throughout her life, Toni has done things her way, always. She sets her mind to something and she becomes completely absorbed. She completes her goals and never looks back. She left little room for a mother. Sometimes it hurts. I have to remember that I taught her that independence; not to need anyone; not to confide in anyone; not to depend on anyone for needs that are yet to be met. She's me. But I always blamed her father because he and I didn't get along." Mrs. Harden lowered her head. Philip reached out just when a tear hit the plate. The tear rolled to the edge of her pasta.

"Why don't they speak?" Philip questioned.

"Toni remembers all the bad events of her childhood vividly. She remembers that he never apologized for what he did or didn't do. Their last fight about the funeral was probably the last straw for her. Knowing Toni like I do, she decided she made it this far without him, now it doesn't matter." Tears streamed down her face. Philip offered her his handkerchief.

She continued, "It doesn't surprise me that he isn't walking her down the aisle. She feels that is an honor which he doesn't deserve."

"I see."

"Philip, Toni will be a good wife. She has prepared for this time in her life. She will certainly try not to repeat the mistakes the rest of us made. You mean a lot to her. She loves you." Mrs. Harden stifled her tears.

"How do you know?"

"My daughter is about action. Her love is based on action. Her actions speak volumes about her love for you."

Mrs. Harden raised her eyes to Philip. At that moment, he knew that he loved Toni deeper than he thought he ever could. He could see Toni in the depths of her mother's eyes.

When he dropped Mrs. Harden at her home, she said something that made him realize that the special woman that he loved was extremely precious.

"Philip, Toni needs the love and attention that I never gave her the way she needed it. She needs to be nurtured even though she has an emotional front around her. I love her. She will need to be held. Please, never hurt her. You'll live to regret it. I do."

He hugged Toni's mom harder than he had intended. He didn't know firsthand what she was feeling and he knew that he never wanted to know. He knew that Toni needed intense passion and he planned to give it to her. He knew that he was ready to love his bride for a lifetime. He knew that he wanted to hug her right now.

Chapter twenty-five

"Please remain seated as the bride enters. Ms. Antoinette Milena Harden." Poised at the back of the church waiting to enter, her coordinator cued her. Toni flowed effortlessly down the aisle.

Elegance in its purest form. Beads, pearls and lace decorated her floor length golden gown. At her wrists, a double row of delicate pearls accentuated the sleeves. She insisted on wearing the matching gold gloves even though they couldn't be seen when she held the bouquet. The bodice sparkled as she glided down the aisle. The same double pearled rows trimmed the neckline to the tip of the V in the back and the hem of the dress including the split. The gown represented marriage; the excellence of a union. The audience was awestruck.

Toni arrived midway of the 50-foot aisle and made eye contact with several guests beyond the protection of her formal veil. The veil's front touched the top of bouquet and the back trailed her by two feet. The golden dye of the veil complemented her gown's elegance. The tiara affirmed her regal aura. The colorless rhinestones reflected the flame from the alter candles as she approached the steps.

The fragrance of the flowers wafted over the audience. Each bridesmaid held a single Calla lily with gold and ivory ribbons. A calla lily and rose arrangement decorated each pew. Her mother and grandmother and Philip's aunt each wore an orchid. There were huge arrangements of white stargazers, tulips and many other flowers surrounded the altar. Like the other pieces, Toni's bouquet combined white blush flowers, a plethora of roses, accompanied by one each of stargazer, orchid, calla lily, tulip and a white Gerber daisy, which centered the arrangement, heavily accented with fern greenery and ivory ribbons.

Toni held her bouquet tightly as she reached her mother's pew. She stopped and curtsied then kissed her mother. The tears slid from her mother's face onto the flowers in Toni's bouquet. Toni reached the altar where Darius waited to assist her up the stairs. Darius stood next to her and held her elbow until the minister asked who gives this woman away. Her mother, Jelly and Darius said, "I do" in unison.

Her elegance stole Philip's breath. He knelt and kissed her gloved hand before moving to her side. Philip faced the minister while he spoke, then turned to Toni to share their vows. Philip couldn't fathom that this day had finally come. The bride of his dreams stood right before his eyes. His spirit settled with assurance of his lifelong mate. His soul mate.

Darius sang beautiful melodies of all of Toni and Philip's favorite gospel songs. Philip's cousin accompanied Darius on the piano, his niece on the harp, his fraternity brother on the saxophone and Jelly's niece on the flute.

As Darius completed "The Lord's Prayer," Toni and Philip walked down the aisle as husband and wife. Midway down the aisle, Toni nearly pulled Philip down jumping the broom. The audience applauded wildly.

She didn't believe her eyes. She did a double take and looked into the eyes of Kennedy. Her past was in this room too strongly for even her to endure. A million thoughts flashed across her mind.

Before she could look at Kennedy a third time, George stood at the church doors. She hadn't seen her play brother since she graduated from high school. She winked to let him know that she saw him.

Sunlight streamed across the tables of the museum's ballroom. The centerpieces resembled the florals at the church. The newlyweds' table bore a full vase of blush colored gerbera daisies and white tulips.

"Attention. Attention. Please join me in congratulating the newlyweds. As the best man and best friend of the groom, I would like to take this opportunity to wish them the best of marriage. Toni, if you have any trouble from him, please let us know and we will straighten him out." The guests let out a loud laugh as they raised their glasses.

Jelly approached him so that she could toast the couple. "Congratulations are not enough to express how happy I am for you both. To have found love in another when there seems to be such chaos around us. To extend those findings to be able to share that love and then multiply it and then apply it to a marriage. That may have renewed my faith in relationships and elevated it back to the miracle it was once considered." Jelly embraced them both.

"To the bride, please love my brother; to my brother, please love your loving bride more than thine ownself. To the both of you, keep God before you and as you grow toward Him, you will grow closer to each other. Remember the triangular relationship." His sister used Toni's words.

Toni was still teary eyed when Darius stood. She knew that the tears would never stop now. "Philip, may she forever enlighten your life, as she has mine and many others. And whatever you did to entice her to fall in love with you, keep doing it. Toni, may happiness forever be at your fingertips and please enjoy peace and tranquility as often as possible. I love you both."

The reception was phenomenal. Philip was extremely serious about the music, and Toni hidden behind her well-earned socialite title made for an excellent "party-giving" couple. The reception was well planned from their arrival to their departure and every possible detail in between until she spotted her father while they were cutting the cake.

He was off in a far corner of the room. It had been so many years since she had seen him. She would not have guessed that she would recognize him. But why wouldn't she, he was still the same man. He stood a lanky 6'1" with weight that often dropped to dangerous levels when he hadn't been taking care of himself. He was diagnosed with diabetes when Toni was six weeks old. His features certainly hadn't changed. His lips were thin, like hers and his hair was still baby-fine and sprinkled with gray, except now he wore it shorter. He was still handsome, too.

He stood there leaning on the wall as if he were watching his favorite movie play right before his eyes. She couldn't see that well because her new contacts were still wearing on her but she thought that he was smiling.

They stopped speaking when she was in college. She wasn't coming home for the summer. She stood her ground even though it hurt and told him no. He slammed the phone down and she never heard from him again: not even when her great-grandmother died.

Her anger reached new heights when she found out that her great-grandmother had died. Through the newspaper, no less. Her mother's friend read the obituaries daily. Toni questioned herself over and over about why he couldn't pick up the phone and call to say that she was ill much less that she was dying. She has never really gotten past that point.

Toni and her father argued over whom was making the final arrangements. Her grandmother finally told him to let Toni, especially since they saw how angry she was because no one bothered to say that she was so ill. When her great-grandfather died, she couldn't find him. She had Jackie call several times to no avail.

She was so involved in her thoughts that she dropped the cake that she going to feed Philip. She looked down; no damage was done to their clothes. She looked up at Philip. He pulled her close to his body in hopes to comfort whatever was plaguing her. She looked over Philip's shoulder and he was gone.

She found herself wishing that she could dance the father/daughter dance with him, although he had done nothing to deserve the honor, let alone the title.

Philip isolated Toni, making it hard for their guests to reach her. He held a plate in front of her hoping that eating would settle that horrified look that he witnessed earlier. He didn't know what ghost she saw but he was determined to find out.

Philip surveyed the room so he could get a clue about who or even what she saw. He was certain that he knew at least one person in each couple. The only people that seemed to be strangers were two men, one of which was medium height, stocky build and accompanied by a nervous looking woman. The other was taller, older, slimmer and alone. Neither of them seemed to know anyone, which seemed somewhat strange as well.

He noticed her mood lighten when she saw her old high school pal. He remembered that George looked out for her in high school. George was even going to fight some guy because he found out that the guy kissed some other girl at the school and Toni saw them.

Toni's line sisters came over so Philip left her to them since she seemed better. He decided to find out what the strange couple was up to first.

"Jelly, do you know those people?" Philip glanced over casually so that only Jelly would know.

"That's Kennedy. Her ex prior to Jon. He's so insecure. You can only imagine that he couldn't handle Toni's lifestyle. Anyway, I'm not sure how he got in but I want to know.

I have considered asking him to leave. I was hoping that she hadn't seen him."

"Do you think that she would've been real startled by seeing him?"

"No, but seeing him would've startled her." Jelly pointed to the older man.

"Who is he?" Philip's brows moved together in bewilderment.

"Her real father."

Jelly stared at Philip wondering what his next move would be.

"Jelly, you need to be near her so that she doesn't look for me. Get Darius and you two keep her occupied." Philip looked around then started his approach.

"Excuse me. May I please have this dance?"

Toni eased around to see George kneeling at her feet. She pulled him up to his feet and graciously obliged.

"So how are you?" Toni asked.

"I'm great actually. I'm getting married in a few months. I've been divorced and have two children, one of each."

"Where is she? Is she here?" Toni's voice escalated with excitement.

He pointed toward their table, "She's over there. I finished school with a masters in accounting. The CPA exam is in a few weeks. This is the first time that we've been out in weeks."

"How did you hear about the wedding?" She was curious.

"You know our high school grapevine is still rampant." He let out a hearty chuckle.

"Excuse me. Can you step outside with me?" Philip looked Toni's dad in the eyes.

He seemed startled. He thought no one would see him much less recognize him. "Okay. Philip is it?" He tried to extend his hand but Philip had already walked ahead of him to the lobby.

"Sir, with all due respect, why are you here?" Philip rested his hands on the ledge.

"Let's sit over here, please. Philip, I came because I love my daughter. I really wanted to be back in her life. I miss her alot. You can only imagine how I felt when I heard that she was getting married. She didn't call; nor did she send an invitation. I knew that I had been unfair and that not speaking to my child was wrong. I want to make amends. I want her to be happy, and I want to be there for her. I miss hugging my little girl, though she's not a little girl anymore."

"Right now is not a good time to speak with her. I want you to call me next week. I'll see what I can do. Here's my card. I do have a favor to ask; I think you should leave. I don't think that this is appropriate." Philip looked over to the wedding party. "Look, it's time for me to dance with my bride. It's nice to have met you."

Philip watched her father leave. He seemed so sad, but Philip had no choice. Toni would be so distraught. So many issues and emotions would rush back. He decided that he would bring it up when they returned home from the honeymoon.

Philip took Toni's hand from George's. He spun her like she was Cinderella. He never wanted this high to leave. He had lived his dream of marriage to the woman that was his soulmate and best friend. She encouraged him to extend his focus, to expand his comfort zone, and to do great things. He was more invigorated now than ever about his career, the museum and the fraternity, all because Toni supported and encouraged him. She truly inspired him.

"I love you." He whispered in her ear.

Chapter twenty-six

As they rode in the limo to the airport, she sounded frightened. "Did you see my father? He was at the reception. I wish he had spoken."

She seemed content enough to have said those things. "I spoke to your father Toni." Now he realized why she dropped her plate. Her dad was her ghost. "What do you want to do about him?"

"Eventually, we'll speak. What did he say to you?"

"I'd better let him tell you. He shared his feelings, a little. He apologized. He said that he read the newspaper announcement. I gave him my card; told him to call me in two weeks. I was going to bring it up on the way home. I really just want you to relax for the next week."

"I love you, Philip."

"I love you, Toni." He heard those words as if she had said them for the very first time. They held such new meaning.

"Dr. Harden speaking."

"Finally, I hear your voice. You're still beautiful, Toni. You were simply gorgeous. I never thought that I would see the day that you would marry another man."

"Kennedy, it's nice to hear from you, too. I assume you enjoyed the wedding and reception." Toni tapped her pen on her desk.

"Yes, I did. Congratulations on the wedding. I would've spoken at the reception but Jelly ask me to leave so I decided to call today, figuring that you would be back from your honeymoon. I was quite impressed with the museum. I was hoping that you would be able to assist me with becoming a member."

She flipped through her planner to jot some notes. "Well Kennedy, as usual your timing needs some fine tuning. At any rate, museum memberships are available by calling and someone will fax you the information you need. Thank you for your well wishes. I am truly happy. I wish that I had known Jelly asked you to leave. It should not have been a problem."

"You know that she's very protective of you and to top that off she dislikes me. I expected it. She was civil, though. I just called to wish you the best. I told Angelica how lucky Philip is to have you. How much I miss you. Thank you for making me the man that I am. Thank you for helping me reach my level."

"Good afternoon, Kennedy." Toni returned the phone to the cradle.

Kennedy had not been the best mate she ever had. She was ending that relationship when she met Jon. It was a harsher breakup than it needed to be. He was in love with her but the feeling was less than mutual. One-sided relationships always end. They met in high school and the relationship lasted through the summer after her senior year. It finally ended when he missed their first date's anniversary and tried to make up for it. He came to her house in an attempt to surprise her. When he arrived, she was leaving for dinner with Jon. He seemed devastated, but Toni found that hard to believe since she had heard from one of her friends at school that he was seen regularly with the same young lady from another school. It was also rumored that they had slept together. Since Toni wasn't into the relationship, she found this a good reason to let it go.

"Dr. T, your 3 o'clock is here." Daphne spoke into the intercom.

"Send them in, please. Thank you." Toni came from behind her desk to greet her new patient.

Daphne opened the door, and a little person ran to her. She reached down just in time to scoop up the thirteen-month old little girl. The gold stud earrings were the biggest clue and her smile was the next. Toni looked up and saw George. She had hoped that she would see him after the reception and here he was.

"Girl, do you know how much I missed you? I've wanted to call but couldn't get a hold of you. Other than newly and happily married, how are you?"

"I'm fine. The question should be how are you? And what is this darling's name?"

"Krishan is the younger of the two. George III is at school today. He's five. Their mother and I were married for three years. The longest three years of my life. The divorce was messy, but the children ended up with me, and I absolutely love it. I'll be married in a month."

"Congratulations. Let me know if I can do anything to help. I'm real sorry about your divorce. But it looks like you got the better end of the deal. Your daughter is precious. Tell me about the fiancée."

"Her name is Danielle. She has been a blessing. Anyway, my dad said hello too. The reason that we are here is because they need a pediatrician. Danielle saw your bridal picture in the paper for the clinic and your service to the community. She had made this appointment before we went to the wedding. I didn't realize you were one in the same. She didn't show me the photo and the article until after the wedding when she realized that it was you. And she saw the museum's article, too. I never paid a lot of attention because I thought you were going to be an attorney and eventually a judge, so I never put two and two together."

Kris hopped down to the Lego table while they talked. She was truly a precious baby. She reminded Toni of herself when she was that age.

"Well, let's examine this young lady. When will you be bringing your son to see me?"

"He'll be here later today. Danielle is bringing him."

Toni walked Kris to the exam room. Kris was very attentive to Toni as she moved around. She was real excited when she heard her father's heartbeat with the stethoscope. Back in her office, she completed her notes and sat with Krishan to talk to George.

"I'll send a request for her records if you don't have a copy. She's a healthy baby. She'll just need a check-up in six months unless she has any problems between now and then. She's a cutie, too."

Kris was holding on to Toni's jacket attempting to maintain her balance as she stood on the sofa. She tried to touch the pictures on the wall behind them. They were so busy talking they didn't hear George III come into the room. Kris jumped down to hug her brother. Daphne followed Danielle into the office. Daphne offered them something to drink, as she scooped Kris up to go to the reception area to play.

"Excuse us, we'll be in Exam #3." Toni walked George III to the exam room.

Once there, George III listened to Toni's heart. They were both so well behaved. They made her want a child of her own. She and Philip were only newlyweds though. They returned to her office.

"It's nice to finally meet you." Toni reached to hug Danielle.

"It's great to meet you. I've had to hear so much about you since the wedding. I've heard more about high school than I have since I met him." Danielle smiled widely.

"Congratulations. You have access to a wonderful man."

"Thank you. Congratulations to you. I brought your invitation. How was the honeymoon?"

"It was awesome. It was great to relax." Toni prepared to leave. Her staff had been gone thirty minutes.

Chapter twenty-seven

"Look, with all due respect, you owe your daughter a lot; a lot of explanation, a lot of love, a lot of everything. You left her in a time of need. She has been through a lot since then. You had no right to hold her responsible for that nonsense."

"Philip, I know. I'm sorry. I don't know how to approach her. She stared at me at the reception like she didn't know me. It felt like she was looking right through me."

"She does have quite a bit going on. We just moved together. We have the museum to see after, our medical practices, we each have our hobbies and community activities. She needs you. She loves you." Philip ran his index finger along the rim of his cognac glass. "I'll arrange for her to talk to you. I'll help you if you don't hurt her."

"I was wrong, Philip. I miss my little girl. I would've given anything to give her away at her wedding. Anything. Do you think that she'll talk to me?"

"I'm going to give it my best."

"How did she do when my grandfather died?" Toni's father spoke barely above a whisper.

"She needed you. She was Toni, strong, hiding her feelings. Exterior like Fort Knox. Interior soft as bread. She's a lovely woman. She grew up with a strong female support group, but she was daddy's little girl first. She missed the way you used to hold her when she was a little girl. You were supposed to be there for her."

"I know. Thank you, Philip, for all your help. I really need to talk to her. I know that there is nothing that I can do to make up the time that I've missed in her life."

"Come to our house tomorrow about seven. We'll have dinner and you two can talk. You have to give her time to adjust to having you return to her life. So be patient and don't rush anything."

Philip left Toni's father at the brownstone where they had happy hour drinks. Philip needed to hurry to talk to Toni if this dinner was to go smoothly tomorrow.

♦ ♦ ♦ ♦ ♦

"Sweetheart, I missed you. How was your day?" Philip entered their home. He couldn't convince Toni to buy a new house, or move for that matter.

She tried to compromise, but he knew that she had been there only a few months and he knew what an accomplishment building a home was. He had been moving in somewhat slowly after the wedding. He finally completed moving the big items, like electronics and clothes. He and Toni could move and buy something together later.

Toni rose to meet him at the foyer. They embraced and kissed, passionately. For some reason, the ceremony just publicized the union that already existed in their hearts.

"I missed you, too. My day was fine and yours?"

"My day was rather interesting. Tell me about yours." Philip fished for the perfect time to tell her about their special dinner guest.

"I saw my high school brother George today. Remember I danced with him at the reception. Well, I am their pediatrician now. He has a boy and a girl. He's getting married the same day as Jennifer. Anyway, I invited them to dinner tomorrow. I'm sorry I did not check your calendar. I really want us to have dinner with them. I was thinking of Fettuccini Alfredo with chicken and a salad."

Philip led her to the sofa and Bubbles hopped in her lap. "Sweetheart that's fine. I sort of planned a surprise for tomorrow night, but I'll move my surprise to early afternoon. I'll meet you at your office tomorrow after 3:30 PM."

♦ ♦ ♦ ♦ ♦

"Jackie, pencil Philip in for 3:30 PM please."

"Too late, he's already here."

"Send him in." She came from around her desk because she figured that it was Philip and she wanted a hug. She had looked forward to his visit.

He stepped in the room and closed the door behind himself. "I have a surprise for you and I want you to understand that my intentions are the best. Have a seat."

He made her nervous. She remained in the seat where he left her with her back to the door. She would just as easily been blind folded because they eased in so quietly that they were both before her before she knew it.

She stood up and put her hand over her mouth, then over her eyes and then returned them back to her mouth. She lowered her petite frame into the chair on top of her hands. Her eyes rolled to the floor. She leaned back and placed her hands in her lap. She fidgeted a bit longer. She played with her earrings. She curled her hair between her thumb and forefinger like she does when she's sleepy. A single tear rolled down her cheek. She sat forward and placed her face in her hands.

Philip kneeled down to comfort her. He offered her his handkerchief.

"This is deeper than what I knew. Had I known, darling, I would have never done this without speaking to you first. I'm so sorry." He held her. He felt her stifling her tears.

She pulled away from Philip and paced the floor. She had to pull her emotions together. She was seeing her father for the first time in six years. This was indeed the same man that was at her reception. She searched the floor for a starting place. She had to form words that accurately expressed her feelings. It was probably best that Philip hadn't told her. She probably would have never let them come. But he was here now. Philip had his head in his hands and was sitting behind her desk. Her father was just sitting there on the chair facing where she had initially sat. Finally, she spoke.

"Hello. How are you?"

"You've grown to be a beautiful woman. I couldn't believe it when I saw your picture in the paper. The wedding was beautiful. You seem very happy. I just stopped by to apologize for the father that I never was. I want you to know that I love you and miss you. I think of you daily. I know..."

Toni's tears soaked her blouse. She cut him off with a hint of anger in her voice. "You don't know what it means to grow up in the same city and know that I can't come to you when it counts. I wasn't "Daddy's little girl" anymore because Daddy quit! At times that I needed you most, you were nowhere, absolutely nowhere to be found. On top of that, in your absence, you were absolutely hateful. That dispute was between Mother and you, not me. Even when I had good news, I couldn't call you either. I couldn't call you when I really thought that a "daddy" was appropriate. You haven't been speaking to me during my most major challenges and triumphs. You selfish asshole! Why did you bring me into this world if you weren't going to love me, always? I was never a bad child. I was never an embarrassment. What happened?"

Philip decided that was more of a rhetorical question being that she had flopped down on the leather sofa sobbing. Philip knelt in front of her to hold and comfort her. Her sobs only got louder when she felt his touch.

"Antoinette, I'm sorry. I didn't mean to leave you. I don't want to hurt you."

She cut him off again, shouting, "I buried my great-grandfather alone. I nearly buried my great-grandmother alone too."

"Look, sir. I made a mistake by bringing you here. I think you'd better go." Philip left her side to escort him out. This had not turned out the way he expected. She was more upset than he realized. How could he have been so distracted as to believe that her seeing her father could be the best thing for her now? How could he be so presumptuous that she wanted to or that she was ready to face him?

A million thoughts rushed through her mind. A million feelings rushed through her body. She knew how it felt to be rejected. She didn't want to continue this forever. Maybe they could work on being friends. He wouldn't be able to be her father, but he could be her friend. He probably needed this more than she did.

"Wait. Wait. Don't leave. I've been angry for so long until I didn't know what else to say. I miss you, too. You just don't know what it feels like to need someone and no one is there. When I finally have a soul mate-confidant, he has to absorb all of this." She pulled Philip back to her and he held her tightly.

Then for the first time in years, her father held her in his arms like she was a little girl again. She felt so safe, so secure. Only Philip felt better. Her body jerked with sobs. She stood there in his arms for what seemed like eons. Her sobs finally stopped. She stood back and looked at him. She remembered him exactly. She wondered if he was taking care of himself. His diabetes was known to be out of control at various points in his life.

Philip stood closely behind her. He felt better now. "Why don't we go eat? You're hungry right?"

"Yeah, I am, as a matter of fact."

"We better hurry. George and Danielle will be at our house in about an hour and I have cooked nothing." She felt better, lighter, more at ease.

She kissed Philip and they promised to meet at home. She decided to invite Jelly, Darius, Martin and Julia if they could make it. She could have the little restaurant around the corner deliver some dinner.

"Darius, I couldn't believe that he was standing in front of me after all those years. He watched me get married. He was actually there."

Everyone had gone. Darius hung around to talk to her. It had been awhile since they had a heart-to-heart. They were sipping wine in the dining room.

"Are you okay?" Darius leaned back and crossed his long legs.

"I'm better now that I shared with him all that anger that I had suppressed for so long. I released all that stress. He listened, too. It was like he knew that it was going to happen. We both cried. I scared Philip. I showed him more emotion tonight than I ever had. He didn't realize that I had hidden my feelings like that. Anyway, I think that my father and I can be friends." She leaned against the counter in the kitchen.

"I hope so. I'm glad it finally happened."

"Me too," Toni said.

"Hey, I like George and Danielle. I think that they make a great couple. When is their wedding?"

"In a month. The same day as Jennifer's."

"I'd like to go."

"I'm sure that they wouldn't mind. Are you bringing Julia?"

"Yes, I may be proposing soon. She is better to me than I realized. She's more independent than I thought, too. Either I didn't take her seriously or I simply was not listening. She just closed on a home. She just signed a deal to open a bookstore and art gallery. She still does trading on the Dow. She reminds me of you. She says stuff once and when she says it, it's nearly done. She's actually the one. She just hid a lot from me or something. Anyway, I want to go to St. John's for Labor Day. Should I get two tickets for you two?"

"Let me check with my sweetie. I'll get back to you." Toni started twirling her hair.

As she felt warm hands on her neck, Philip spoke softly. "Sweetie, that should be fine. Sure, Darius go ahead and order our tickets. Call my office tomorrow and have Cameron cut you a check."

"No problem, man. I'll call you both with the final plans. I'll talk to you tomorrow." Darius grabbed his blazer off of the rack and headed for the door.

"Hey man, don't get so caught up in Darius that you forget that other people care, too. Don't overlook her—you'll live to regret it. I promise. Be careful. Goodnight." Philip spoke confidently.

When she closed the door, her husband, her family, was waiting for her at the base of the stairs. He scooped her into his arms and carried her up the stairs with ease. He placed her on the wrought iron sleigh bed. He showered her with kisses. He ignited an indescribable passion.

He lowered his body onto hers. Her long sighs were just the indication that he needed to continue to taunt her body with his powerful body language. She drew him close and held him tightly. He escalated her passion to the next level. They moved in sync until they both exploded. She wrote I love you on his chest.

He rubbed her hair until she let out a soft snore. He held her close. She was always so warm. He loved her so much. He hadn't intended to see her sad nor upset with her father. She had been his savior. She was the woman he had prayed for. She took his breath away. He thought of everything that he needs to keep her, not simply happy, but ecstatic. He envisioned the rest of his life with this awesome and loving woman. He drifted off dreaming of his wonderful wife and marriage.

Chapter twenty-eight

Toni duplicated her bridal luncheon exactly for Jennifer. She overheard Jen talking to Kiki about the wedding plans. Jen didn't know that Toni planned her bridal luncheon. Between Jackie and Daphne, they planned to surprise her. Toni arranged for the bridesmaids and her mother to be picked up by a limo and brought to the luncheon.

The hostess led Jen, Jackie, and Daphne down the stairs to the Wine Room of Charlie's 517. Jen turned the corner. "Surprise!" Her eyes lit up.

"I should've known that you were behind all of this." She blushed. They seated her at the middle of table with her mother and her best friend on either side. Jen admired the pink and ivory balloon bouquets at each corner and at either end of the table.

"I had no idea, Dr. T. Thank you."

Toni always wanted her staff to know she cares about what goes on beyond the walls of the office in their own worlds. This occasion was no different. They served the dinner French style. The chef prepared a special Cajun chicken with fresh green beans and the special corn, the cream mixed with whole kernel with a pinch of sugar. Only Toni could bring the flavor and variety of home cooking, while in one of Houston's finest restaurants.

Jen was completely outdone when the server rolled dessert into the room. He served everyone's favorite: strawberry shortcake.

They mingled and played a few shower games. But mostly they talked about what they didn't want in a marriage, what they wished for, which of course, was different from what they decided that they would settle for. They chuckled really hard when Toni confessed that her wishes come true daily. They all found it hard to believe that Philip could actually bring more to her life than what she already had. A couple of them felt envy of her relationship and sometimes her life. They never felt that she flaunted her possessions. She openly displayed her feelings, and emotions about Philip and sometimes herself. They wanted to experience the same things.

"Jen, your gift." Toni removed the cover from the easel unveiling the 32" x 40" hand painted portrait of Jen and her groom. Her elation turned into tears by the time she touched the portrait. Toni smiled. She thought they would never part. Toni remembered how she felt at her bridal luncheon. Jen was equally as ecstatic.

Toni and Philip rushed to Danielle and George's nuptials. Just as they were seated on the groom's side, George's youngest brother asked to speak with her. She went to the foyer of the church with Angelo. He delivered a message from Danielle. Toni asked if Danielle wanted to see her. He said that she could see Danielle but that Toni might want to find the coordinator, instead.

He found Toni first and asked her to sit near the front next to the stairs. It was about to start. She winked at George when he entered the church. She had forgotten how good he looked in a tuxedo. Today, he was slightly more nervous. This, of course, heightened when Danielle entered the sanctuary. His expression was absolutely priceless. His daughter, Krishan, who was dropping the white rose petals as delicately as possible, preceding Danielle. She kept looking over her shoulder as if to be sure that Danielle was still following her. When she finally reached her father, she dropped several petals where she thought Danielle would stand. She looked back once more. Then she put some more at her father's feet. George bent to kiss her and she kissed and hugged him back. Her petals fell from her basket over his shoulder. She let him go and turned to be sure that Danielle was right there. Krishan crossed the path once more, blowing Danielle a kiss through her gloved hand, on her way to her seat.

George reached for Danielle and eased her next to him as if they would stand there forever. There was a pause. Toni nearly missed her cue. The musician played the introduction and when Toni actually got to the microphone, he was almost done. George had been looking into Danielle's eyes and the details of her veil and the shoulders of her dress before he turned around to the sound of Toni's voice. Danielle's mission had been completed. He wanted to ask her but wasn't sure how she would respond. Danielle could tell that he was happy to hear her sing, and "The Lord's Prayer" no less. He looked back at Danielle with excitement. Toni winked at Danielle behind his back. Toni took her seat next to Philip not realizing that she would be singing later.

The ceremony was beautiful. George matched her surprise by writing his own vows. When he started, she thought that he had forgotten the ones that they practiced. This would be hard to top, but they each tried.

Chapter twenty-nine

"I didn't know that you were going to sing." Philip opened her door.

"I didn't either. She heard him talking about my singing. She decided but hadn't had chance to ask without him knowing. I'm glad she asked. At the same time, I'm glad that Jen didn't ask. I would've probably cried. Anyway, Jen's ceremony was gorgeous. There ought to be a law that if you have overlapping guests with someone else, your nuptials cannot be on the same day. I'm exhausted" Toni chuckled and rested on the headrest. She allowed the smooth sounds of Boney James to soothe her.

Her own marriage had been in transition. They've been settling in. She thought that he only moved in with her because he didn't have the heart to ask her to move with him because she had just built the house. He seemed comfortable enough or that's the impression that he gave. He had taken on various duties. She remembered their first little fight. He wanted to know where mortgage coupons were. He caught her off guard. She nearly snapped.

"Why do you want those?"

"So that I can pay it when I pay the rest of the bills. Oh, and where are those, too?" The look on her face assured him that she was shocked.

"That's part of what I'd like to do in our marriage. Did you think that this would never happen? It sounds as if the thought never crossed your mind." He was so gentle. He guided her to the sofa and sat her down.

"No, I guess it didn't. I never expected you to pay my bills. The house or otherwise. I'm really sorry. I guess I should've thought of that."

"If it is better, I'll set up an account for the house and you can still pay the bills but out of that account." He took her hands in his.

"It's not that really. I just forgot that part. I don't know how, but I did."

"Well, we have an appointment tomorrow with my attorney so that we can sign my will and a property distribution document. I want you to fill a will as well."

"I have a will." She responded defensively, realizing that she was not prepared, which was certainly a first. "Philip, I'm sorry. I don't know why this is a surprise. I'll get ready for tomorrow."

"Sweetheart, that's okay. This is new for both of us. I just want you to be financially secure if anything happens to me. I am to provide for you. I love you. What I have done is arranged for our attorneys to meet with us. My attorney has prepared my financial statements for your review. My will is updated where you are the beneficiary and executor. All I want you to do is have it."

She wiped her tears away, "I'm so embarrassed."

"Why?"

"I'm not prepared."

"You don't need to be prepared. I've waited so long for this moment. To marry the woman of my dreams and to provide for her needs. You, Toni are that woman. Everything I have belongs to you. I have had plenty of time to prepare for you." Philip enclosed Toni in the circle of his warm embrace.

She had drifted off. The brakes' squeal snapped her out of her daydream. She looked up into the headlights of the oncoming truck. She felt the truck swerve. She closed her eyes for a moment. When she opened them again, they were hit and had run off the road. All Toni could feel was the truck bumping down the hill off which they fell. She looked over at Philip and couldn't see his face but she could tell that he wasn't conscious. She touched his forehead and felt blood.

She tried to reach past Philip's body to get the brakes. She got one foot over there but realized that Philip foot was stuck on the accelerator preventing her from fully depressing the brake. She manipulated his dead weight such that she was finally able to press the brake. The car was dropping out of control. She tried to steer the truck so that she didn't flip.

She finally brought the truck to a stop.

"911. How may we help you?"

"We were just hit and are on the side of the construction of the I-10 freeway on the hill."

"Ma'am, is anyone hurt?"

"My husband is unconscious. He has a faint pulse and is bleeding in several areas." She knew that she couldn't afford to panic. Philip's life depended on her proactive attitude.

"Ma'am, I have already dispatched a unit. Do you know what hit you?"

"All I saw was headlights."

"Ma'am, can I have a name and number where you can be reached?"

"Dr. Antoinette Morris. 555-0562."

"Ma'am, I will call you right back."

She managed to stabilize his neck and head. She couldn't move him much, especially not until help arrived. She heard him try to say something. She hurried to hush him. She found his medical emergency bag. When the EMS team arrived, she gave all his vitals. They were ready to take him away, when the paramedic explained, "Ma'am, can you lay here? We need to check you out too."

"I'm just going with my husband. I'm fine."

"Ma'am, you're forehead is cut."

"We are both doctors. I feel fine."

"You don't have to go on a stretcher but I will check all of your vitals."

"Okay." She responded as she reached for her forehead.

As soon as she was out of the truck, the guy started hoisting the truck onto his wrecker truck. The police were waiting at the top of the ledge. They spoke to her on her way into the ambulance. She noticed an eighteen wheeler with his hazard lights on across the street and the driver was standing in front of it.

"Ma'am, I have some questions."

The paramedic interrupted, "Officers, you have to meet us there— he's critical and she has to go with us."

At the hospital, Philip was admitted as critical. With one phone call from the ambulance, his sister, Cameron, Jackie, her mother, Jelly and Darius were at the hospital when she arrived. They kept her overnight for observation. She wanted to be at Philip's bedside, so they had to put her in ICU, too. She couldn't believe this had happened.

She went home the next day and prepared for Philip's return. She sat down to rest and drifted off with thoughts of Philip in her mind. The accident was related to diabetes. His low blood sugar caused him to black out. Philip's doctor informed Toni that he was now diabetic and would be on medication for the rest of his life. His diet wouldn't be severely modified, but changed nonetheless. They could handle it though. They were doctors. They saw it everyday. Before she dealt with that, they had injuries to deal with. When Darius brought her home, Philip was still listed in critical condition yet stable and still in ICU. He wasn't breathing independently. He was also on a heart monitor as a precaution.

The phone brought her out of her daydream.

"Baby, I'm on my way to get you. They want to take Philip to surgery and they need your signature." Jelly's nervousness flowed through the phone.

"Okay, Jelly. I'll be ready when you get here. By the way, did they say why?" Toni only heard a dial tone in response.

Philip looked so pale she almost didn't permit the surgery. She knew that he would struggle but he needed it.

Sixteen hours later, she finally crawled into her bed at home once again. This time Jelly stayed with her. She wanted to stay at the hospital but the ER doctor wouldn't let her. It was obvious that she was exhausted. The doctor sent her home with some pain medication. She slept for a few hours until the telephone rang. She picked it up but Jelly had it. She vaguely heard her niece's voice.

"Aunt Jelly, I have to speak to her. My father said she was hurt in the accident. I need to see her. Please. Aunt Jelly. I'm worried. How's Uncle Philip?" Khayla heaved a heavy sigh. Toni thought she heard her crying.

"Khayla, sweetie. Your aunt is sleeping. Your uncle is in critical but stable condition. That means that they are going to watch him closely. He ..."

"I know what it means, Aunt Jelly. Can you come get me?"

"Yes, Sweetie. I will be there shortly. Where is your father?" Jelly asked that question knowing full well that Khayla didn't really care.

Something else was wrong though. When Toni put the phone down, she could tell that although her niece was worried, there was something else. She couldn't quite put her finger on it.

"Jelly wait. Where's my mother?" Toni startled Jelly as she entered the kitchen.

"She's at the hospital. I told her to stay and I would stay with you. Darius went home for awhile to meet Julia. We sent Philip's sister home. She was a wreck. I'm going to get Khayla. I guess she'll spend the night. She's got something happening. By the way, you've got several messages on the bar. See ya in a few."

"Jelly, make my mother go home, please. Be careful."

Toni answered the phone on the first ring. "Hello."

"Toni, what are you doing, sweetie?" Darius spoke in a low tone.

"Khayla called and coaxed Jelly into going to get her."

"I'm surprised that you're up. Look, Julia and I are going to stay at the hospital tonight. Cameron picked up your mother and took her to eat and then will drop her at home. We'll call you if anything changes."

"Hold on D, the door bell's ringing."

"Well there's my daughter." Her mother walked in looking beat. Cameron followed her. He blushed slightly.

"D, let me call you back. Mother has just walked in."

"Mother, thank you for staying at the hospital for me. You have no idea what this means to me. Cameron, did she eat?"

"She ate a little bit. She picked over her food."

"Mom, are you staying with me?"

"Baby, if you need me, I will." She lowered herself onto the sofa.

"Cameron, please take my mother home. How much was dinner?"

"I put it on the office card."

"Just bring the bill to me or Jackie."

"Mrs. Harden, are you ready to go?" Cameron stood in front of her as if she were his own mom.

"Yes, I guess. I just hate to leave Toni."

"Mom, I'm better. Besides, Jelly is coming back with Khayla. Then I'm going to the hospital until Philip is better and able to come home."

Toni and her mom hugged as they left. Jelly and Khayla walked into the kitchen just as she shut the door. Jelly parked in the garage. The truck was in the body shop. The insurance company had already called for her statement. The wheels were in full motion for the truck to be fixed. There was a lot of under-carriage damage. The driver admitted that he was at fault for making such a wide turn. The adjuster said that it would be ready in a few days. Jelly said the rental car was delivered that same afternoon.

"Auntie, I'm glad that you're okay." The 15 year-old child, seemingly a mirror image of Toni reached for her and held her tightly. Toni cringed under her embrace, as her muscles still ached a bit.

Khayla had experienced the same thing that all teens do: that awkwardness and distance between her and her parents. So she had confided in her Aunt Toni about most everything. They became closer when Toni started her practice. She needed Toni because although Toni understood both sides, she talked to Khayla as if they were friends regardless of age and familial relations. Toni's honesty with Khayla made the difference. Toni remembered when Khayla called her one day and she sounded distant but Toni ignored it.

"Aunt T, can you come take me to the store?" Toni remembered her asking.

"Sure." Toni responded knowing that something was happening.

When they arrived, Khayla maneuvered to the aisle and turned to Toni asking, "Which kind do you recommend?"

Surprised, Toni asked, "For you?"

"It happened this morning." Khayla searched for her aunt's approval.

"That's good. How do you feel?"

"I'm okay. It felt weird."

Toni suggested a few to try and decide after seeing what worked. "I remember when your grandmother made a pretty box for me for storage. We took a grocery box and covered it with contact paper that matched my room. That was years ago. We'll buy you a box. I have just the one in mind."

On the way home, Khayla confessed, "I wish I could share as openly with my mother."

Toni heard the sadness in her voice, "It does get better. I'm still trying to get closer to my mother. It's a process, not a destination. She'll come around. You need to tell her though."

"Thank you for being there for me as usual." Khayla packed her new products to the front door, waving goodbye to Toni.

♦ ♦ ♦ ♦ ♦

"Thank you, Precious. I miss you, too. What's going on?" Toni led her to the living room to have a seat.

"School is going well. I'm going to finish early as I had planned. I finished the packet that you sent and I already mailed it. Rice said that they notify for the spring by October. The University of Houston notifies as they decide. For the summer, I want to go to UH so that I know how distracting college can be, I think. I thought of Houston Baptist University and University St. Thomas, too. Anyway, I'm applying to Rice, Trinity, Stanford, Hampton, and Emory for the fall, maybe the summer. I'm really glad to be graduating in December. My folks really went for the local college thing so that I could go to prom and the other social stuff. They were going to make me stay until I told them it was your idea."

Toni knew there was more to this discussion. But there was time, and if she knew Khayla, she would be here awhile. Besides, this was the first time she had been here since she and Philip got married.

"I'm really excited for you. Have you paid senior dues and your yearbook, yet?"

"Yes, I did. My pictures came back today. I wasn't able to get them though."

Toni noticed that she was wearing two class rings. "Why do you have that boy's class ring?"

"Because he's mine. I have his letterman jacket, too. How is everyone going to know? We don't see each other that much."

"Well, don't forget what we discussed. Anyway, aren't you tired? Did you eat something? Let's go see if Jelly wants something. I'm calling the restaurant up the street." Toni could tell there was something more. Khayla didn't give her normal response and Toni recognized that glow.

♦ ♦ ♦ ♦ ♦

Toni didn't like the doctor's report so she started looking for his chart. She thought, "Where is his chart? It never seems to be around. I want to see it for myself." They brought Darius and Julia some breakfast, who left shortly afterwards. Khayla rode with Jelly to run some errands, grocery shop, and go to Toni's office. Toni was going to try to work the rest of the week. She thought that it would make her feel better. They had rescheduled her clients for the latter part of the week. When they left, she started looking for Philip's chart again.

It seemed strange that the entire hospital staff knew that she was there. Most of them came by and spoke to her. She knew everyone knew when she got a hospital intercom page. The ICU nurse nodded her head when Toni motioned that she would be right back.

She met the chief of surgery in the hospital's boardroom along with the chief of staff. The surgeon explained, "The operation only fixed some things. I want to operate again because Philip is still not breathing independently. The diabetes was interfering with my normal surgical methods. He is also experiencing some abnormal heart rhythms. We are going to keep him sedated until we can fix all of those problems. Toni, we are doing everything we can to get him better as quickly as possible."

Toni was sobbing by this point. The chief of staff placed several documents in front of her. "We need you to sign these. We'll be back."

Her pager persisted. She stopped crying long enough to return the calls. One was the administrative desk. They needed her to sign some papers, and several people were looking for her including Carolyn, Jackie, and Dr. Sessoms, a fellow surgeon of Philip's. The desk directed all of them to the boardroom. The papers were routine insurance and treatment consent. Carolyn rushed to her with a handkerchief.

"Carolyn, please get his chart for me. They won't let me see it. They aren't being straight with me. There is something wrong with my husband and I can't do anything. I am getting frustrated."

"Sweetie, calm down. I'll see what I can do. I've had all of his flowers delivered to your office. As you know, flowers aren't allowed in ICU. They are beautiful, though. I didn't want them wasted."

"I don't care about flowers right now, Carolyn. My husband, my family is in serious condition. I wasn't ready for this."

"Jackie is here." Carolyn stopped as Jackie walked in. She said a few hushed words to Jackie, then left.

"Hey Dr. T. How are you holding up? You look pretty."

Only Jackie would point out how she looked as if nothing was wrong. "Thank you, Jackie. How's the office?"

"I let everyone go home. We'll be there late for the rest of the week. Our pediatric surgeon called and offered to fill in for you if need be. He's in post-op the rest of the week, so he only had rounds in the afternoon, which he could push back. Why don't you let him?"

"I'm about to lose it. I've got to work."

"Okay, but he is on standby. By the way, both of your attorneys will be here shortly. Your attorney called for some information about something else but you know I had to tell him about Philip. Then Philip's attorney called after finally speaking to Cameron. They both said that they were on their way. Cameron came to see me, too. Oh yea, Dr. Sessoms is outside."

"Let him in."

"Toni, everything will be fine. I've got all of his post-ops under control. We've postponed all of his surgeries until we get a status." Dr. Sessoms reached to hug her.

She felt so weak. So nervous. Carolyn came back with food and left again. Dr. Sessoms left, too. Jackie talked some more. She reviewed the items that they covered in staff meeting. "We went out to eat afterwards, though. It wasn't the same. Jennifer is crushed. She called this morning while her husband was playing golf."

"If she calls again, tell her not to worry." Toni spoke as she looked at the food Carolyn brought.

The attorneys arrived at the same time. She thanked Jackie and told her that she would see her tomorrow. Each attorney pulled out several documents. Toni pushed the hospital papers to the middle of the table.

"How are you and how is he?" Philip's attorney spoke first. They both waited intently as she spoke.

"He's heavily sedated. He's not well...." Her voice trailed off in sobs.

"Calm down, Toni. Slow down." He reached for her.

The surgeon returned for his papers. He had never seen Toni this way. He sat across from her at the table.

"Toni, talk to me. What's got you bothered?" The surgeon questioned.

Toni had never felt this weak. Her armor was always in tact. She started again, slowly this time. "Tell me the truth. Is Philip going to make it through the surgery? If not, I won't sign."

Dr. Fred Williams explained to the attorneys the entire procedure, "The purpose is to help him breathe independently. Toni, I can't make any promises about the outcome. The specialist who is coming to operate knows Philip well. We are working hard to save him."

She signed all she could until she reached the page about life support. She moved past that one and signed the rest. "I'll let you know when I can sign the life support. Thank you, Fred."

"The specialist is about two hours away. We will start as soon as he gets here. I'll have someone come get you." He hugged her on his way out.

"What does Philip's living will say about being on life support? I don't remember." Toni's question stung Jeffrey.

He and Philip had grown up together. Only now was he sharing Toni's fears. It hadn't hit him that Philip was really in serious condition. "He's always said no, but he qualified that statement by saying that his family had to make the ultimate decision. That means you, Toni."

"Toni, these documents can wait. These are about the accident. His are about Philip's estate. Man, let's go see Philip. Toni, you didn't eat your lunch. I'll sit with you while you eat. Go ahead man, I'll be right there." Andre sounded disturbed.

"Toni, we're ready to prep." Fred came down personally.

"I didn't expect you. Okay." She was reading to Philip and holding his hand.

"Well, the staff said that they were uncomfortable asking you to leave. Mostly though it was because they know you both and didn't want to upset you." Fred led her into the arms of Darius.

"She can go into the viewing room. She knows how to get there. We're in OR #1."

On the way to the operating room, Khayla and Jelly returned with enough food to feed a small army.

"Aunt Toni, can I speak to you before you go?"

"Sweetie, can it wait?"

"Not really. I wanted to tell you last night but I couldn't find the words." She led Toni to a seat in the hallway.

"What is it baby? I told you that you can always talk to me." She sat facing Khayla as much as possible.

Khayla took Toni's hands into hers. "Aunt Toni, I'm pregnant."

"Oh, Khayla." Toni's tears couldn't be stopped. She could see Darius and Jelly approaching. She held her hand up to stop them. She pulled Khayla close to her and held her tightly. "Sweetheart, let me see your uncle through surgery and we'll discuss this when I return." She kissed her on the forehead.

"There she is. We can start." Fred spoke to Toni with his headset. He forced a smile.

She simply waved. She started to pray when she heard the door open. Darius sat next to her. He explained, "Jelly and Khayla went back to her house, but Jelly may come back later."

Toni wondered, "Where is Philip's sister?"

Darius responded, "I don't know."

"I wonder who is paging me in the hospital. I'll call in a minute." She tossed the paging device aside.

She fell asleep while leaning on Darius. The surgery was still going on when she woke up, except she couldn't hear anything they were saying. Darius was tense and forward with his elbows on his knees.

She dialed the number and they answered, "Maternity." She was puzzled.

"This is Dr. Toni Harden-Morris returning a page."

"This is Nurse Green. Dr. Harden, you have a new niece. Dr. Morris's sister just had her baby. She asked me to page you. That's why she's not in surgery."

"I'll be there soon, okay? Tell her I said congratulations." Toni placed the phone down on the base and sat quietly contemplating life.

Darius stared intently at Philip's fragile body being poked and prodded on the operating table. The door opened slowly with Dr. Fred's assistant standing at the threshold.

"Dr. Harden, will you please come with me?" She took Toni's hand as if they were little girls.

Dr. Fred met them at the doors of the OR. "Toni, we were not able to resuscitate Philip's right lung. It sustained too much damage. We lost him just a few moments ago. I'm sorry."

Chapter thirty

Toni was just tired of funerals. First, her great-grandmother, then her great-grandfather, then Philip's mother, finally her husband. Wasn't there a limit on how many times she had to see this scenario? She got out of the limo and their family, friends and staff stood there with remorse and sympathy for her loss of Philip. She patted her handkerchief in her pocket. She wasn't sure how long she would be able to keep her composure. The number of flowers and cards, telegrams and calls had been overwhelming. She longed to grieve privately.

His Chicago relatives arrived and realized that the circle of life theory had not passed over their family. When each of them got the good news-bad news, they all responded the same—they arrived within two days, extremely supportive.

Toni wanted a private burial but that was totally impossible. Toni's selective memory in regards to their popularity and "fame" escaped her. The church was packed. She should have expected that since it had been full for their wedding. In addition, his death made the front page of several newspapers. There were several celebrities in attendance. Then the mayor arrived. Several local officials also paid homage to Dr. Morris and Dr. Harden- Morris. She had ignored the White House calls. Maybe that wasn't a good idea. She wasn't taken aback until the United States' Surgeon General sat beside her.

Darius sang "The Lord's Prayer" and "His Eye is on the Sparrow." Rev. Allen said a few words. Jelly read a poem. The chief surgeon said a few words. The audience wasn't moved until Toni approached the microphone. She started with "May His Peace Be With You." The choir moved with her as if they had rehearsed. She and Khayla sang "The Battle Is Not Yours." The audience was in tears.

To top that, Toni delivered the eulogy. When the choir stopped humming and she stopped hugging Khayla, she finally started to speak. She was as cold as steel. She hardened her heart to deliver Philip's eulogy.

> "The Lord answers prayers. He answered mine. Each of them. In addition to answering them, He provided me with more than I asked. I'm a successful doctor. I have a house. A car. Food. Clothing. But most importantly, He blessed me with a family. The most recent addition to my life was added on May 14th of this year. A loving man who is my friend, my confidant, my lover, my soul mate…my husband. As I stand before you today, I know that he doesn't prefer this but we as his loved ones have to cope. You have all of the history so I will do what I planned—share some of my personal thoughts about Dr. Philip Morris.

> Dr. Morris—giving and serving his community and his fellow colleagues. He kept his priorities and promises together. He was always available. He, of course, was well liked and admired by his staff and his colleagues, including me. As his wife, I often neglected his importance and meaning to the hospital, and to this nation as a top specialist in his field. I was gently reminded of that fact right before his last surgery. The medical field will greatly suffer because of this loss.

Philip Morris—the community activist. Serving the American Association of Doctors was just par for the course and a small piece of his total commitment. His fraternity will miss him for the guidance and movement that he provided for them and the community, particularly the youth that he affected. I received a telegram from the young men he mentors. They encouraged me to keep my head up and keep his spirit alive by completing his projects and keeping my own focus. Now imagine a group of 13, 14, and 15 year olds encouraging me to pray so that my grief would be easier and bearable. I tried to be strong yet I was extremely touched by their sensitivity.

Opening an African American Museum featuring art, history and culture was more than a task. The Museum has to be the largest community outreach effort yet. The Museum has brought national recognition to our community and more importantly economic sustainability. This monumental feat moved us into the prominent position we need to demand the community support that we deserve.

Philip has touched many lives directly and even more indirectly. He has meant so much to so many people. He meant so much to me, as my husband, my soul mate, my colleague, my family, my friend. I love him so much. We will miss him, but I think I will miss him the most. He brought another dimension to my life—my love life. He made loving him easy.

Now Dr. Philip Morris has passed to another place. Our prayers are with him and all of you who grieve this loss."

The services ended with the audience viewing Philip's resting body. Hundreds of friends, family members and supporters passed and kissed and patted her folded hands. Once they were complete, Toni went to the limo and sat. She was trying to prepare for the burial when his sister interrupted her thoughts.

"Toni, I just want to say thanks for handling all of this for me-for us. My brother's death has been hard on all of us. Please let me know if we can do anything for you." A tear slid past her cheek.

"Thank you. You just care for your baby. That's all I need. Matter of fact I need to start his chart on Monday at the office." Toni forced the smile that everyone expected. Deeper she was not smiling.

The full military burial conjured up the tears that the widow had promised not to display. Dr. Harden-Morris had denied herself the time to grieve that would heal her soul from missing Philip, and to soothe her loss. The strength that she showed with everyone else left her empty at night. But she refused to wallow. She had family that needs her.

Philip's sister ran when they sounded the twenty-one gun military salute in honor of his brief, yet dedicated service to the Marines. Her husband followed. She sat in the limo until the burial ended. Toni watched her until a shadow hovered over her. She followed the shadow from the ground up. The officer addressed her, "Mrs. Philip Morris, thank you for Dr. Morris' contribution to this country," as he presented the flag of the United States of America folded in a tight triangle. He turned and clicked his heels and marched away.

"What was she going to do with a flag in the memory of Philip? Was that supposed to be enough?" Her thoughts upset her.

She closed the door after the last mourner left. Her hands ran through her hair with ease. She pulled the lever on the recliner and stared up at the ceiling. Her life had definitely changed in the last year, but she couldn't deny her blessings.

Philip had brought new meaning to the word joy. They had enhanced each other's lives. She missed him. She knew that nothing lasted forever but she had hoped that it would have been just a little bit longer.

Philip had provided completeness to her life. One that she would never forget. Days filled with passion and energy; intimacy and love. Unforgettable memories that had changed her entire existence.

The ringing phone brought Toni out of her deep state.

"Hello?"

"Aunt T, my dad put me out of the house. Could you please come get me? I'm down the street at Shelly's house."

Toni barely understood Khayla through her sobs. "Khayla, I'll be right there." She grabbed her purse. In the car, she dialed Philip's voice mail to let him know her whereabouts. A rude reality washed over her when the operator came on and referred callers to her office. She slammed the phone down in disgust and disbelief at her loss.

They unloaded her things at the house while they were both still crying.

"What happened?" Toni uttered slowly. It was 10:15 on Saturday night; her niece was about to be a resident of her home.

"I was talking on the phone to Shelly and I was explaining what happened at the funeral and we were just talking. I finally decided to tell her; when mom picked up the phone, I was saying 'pregnant.' Shelly asked me what happened to the condoms that we bought. When I said 'it broke and we kept on going,' that's when I heard mom scream and the phone hit the kitchen floor. I got off of the phone. Dad called me downstairs. He asked. I answered. He told me to leave. I went to Shelly's and then I called you. I could have stayed there but it was only a matter of time before her mother would have found out and that would have been uncomfortable. She doesn't even know why I was really there." Khayla took a deep breath, looking at her aunt awaiting a response.

"Well I'm sure he'll be calling soon. Did you tell him that I know?"

"Yeah. He asked if my boyfriend knew and he does. Aunt T, I was so ashamed. When I told him, he asked me was it his. He said some other stuff like whether or not he could trust me and if I was sleeping with other people. I was so hurt. I couldn't believe that I gave myself to him and he said that he loved me. Aunt T, I believed him." Her speech trailed off into quiet sobs.

Toni reached for her niece. She wanted so much to make it better, but she knew that Khayla's next decision would stay with her for the rest of her life.

Her brother's call interrupted their embrace. "So I guess you know, huh? A parent's nightmare come true."

Toni looked towards Khayla. When their eyes met, a new stream of tears ensued.

She spoke slowly and softly, and eased out of earshot. "She called me to come get her. I'm concerned that she's able to recover from this with as few people knowledgeable as possible. Shelly's mother will be less than receptive if she knows. I don't want that."

"Don't get me wrong sis, I'm not mad at you or what you did. This is just a nightmare. I just wasn't ready to deal with this. Her mother is a wreck."

"Well, I'm going to talk to her then I'll put her to bed. Why don't you come by in about an hour. We'll talk then."

"I messed up huh, Aunt T.?"

"Well, yeah. What's your plan?"

"I can't keep it. I'm not old enough for that. I made a big mistake. Besides, considering my mother's reaction, I don't have much choice." She held her head down.

Toni reached for her chair and held it up. "Was the child conceived out of love?"

"No."

"Will you be able to be civil enough to discuss the child's upbringing?"

"No. He's not returning my calls now as it is."

"Well, I think your decision is clear."

"Is it biblically wrong?" Khayla rolled her eyes to the floor, already knowing the answer.

"Well, everything that has led up to this point has been wrong, but having it won't make it right. Only prayer will fix it."

She led Khayla upstairs to bed and closed the door.

"Aunt T.?"

"Yes, Khayla?"

"Will I ever regret this?"

"Probably, but I'll be right here to support you." She pulled the door behind her and leaned on it for strength.

She brewed some coffee for her brother. She was sipping some tea when he knocked on the door. He hugged Toni until she felt tears. She pulled away from him to look into his eyes. Embarrassed. Hurt. She saw it clearly in his eyes.

"Toni, how is she?"

"She's tired. She hurts. She is embarrassed, too."

He lowered his head. "Where did we go wrong? She's so bright and she's active in church. We give her everything that she needs and wants. What happened?" His voice trailed off.

Toni touched his hand, "You did nothing wrong. You love her. You didn't see this one coming. You missed the signs. She's young and she wanted his acceptance. That has nothing to do with you or your parenting ability. Look, she has learned. She's renewing her self-esteem and her love for self. She knows better now. She wants to be a better child. She wants to get past this and get on the ball with her life. She regained some focus and perspective."

"Thank you. She wasn't going to tell us, was she?"

"No."

"I figured that. How long did you know?"

"She told me right before Philip died. That's when I thought that he wasn't going to make it. Of course, when his sister had her son, he slipped away from me."

"Toni, I'm sorry. I just realized that this is terrible timing for you as well. We did bury Philip fourteen hours ago. I'd better go." He hugged his sister and kissed her on the forehead.

"I'm scared, Toni."

"We'll handle it-trust me." Toni closed the door and leaned on it. A deep breath usually rejuvenated her but not this time.

Chapter thirty-one

"It's been five weeks and I miss Philip—a lot." Toni heaved a weary sigh. Darius' embrace allowed Toni to exhale. The tears slid down her cheek and onto his jacket.

"I know. I know. Look we can postpone this trip. That may be better. We don't have to go now." Darius brushed her hair from her face.

"No, we already have plans. He would want me to go, too. Ooh, I miss him. How do you survive the pain with the memories that we have?"

"Such an explosive and heartfelt love." Darius reflected on their first trip with Philip to Aspen.

Thoughts of their passion made Toni blush. She chuckled out loud.

"I'm almost ready. Just give me a few more minutes. Where is everybody else?" Toni continued to pack.

"Jelly, Martin, and Julia are meeting us at the airport."

The plane touched down in Orlando around 2:00 pm.

"I thought we were going to the islands?" Toni questioned.

"We changed the plans once we convinced you to go. We thought that you would have a better time if you were here. The islands would conjure up too many memories—even for us." Jelly spoke almost laboriously.

The limo whisked them off to the World Center Marriott of Orlando. She surmised that Disneyworld was the new destination.

"I'm glad I brought my camera," Toni teased in protest of the change of plans.

"We're just glad you're here." Martin touched her shoulder.

Julia held her hand, "We miss you. I haven't seen you in a while. You okay?"

"Yes. I take it one step at a time and day by day. I was telling Darius this morning that I miss him still but I pray daily. I've tried to be business as usual, probably so that I don't concentrate on missing him. The museum keeps me the busiest. We are selecting a new board chair since I became the chair of the trustee board. The fundraisers and planning keep me busy. I just completed my manuscript. The office is busy because school starts next week." She heaved a heavy sigh. "Well, this'll be fun. Probably just what I need." Her voice trailed off.

"Look no more sad talk. We are here to have a great time. We are almost to the hotel. Look!" As high spirited as Jelly was, she was not about to let the group lose their focus.

"Dinner is at 6:00 pm in the Amethyst Room. Don't be late." Julia pushed the elevator button and looked around at their faces. She stopped at Toni. "Call me if you need anything."

Dinner started with smoked salmon and dill relish sauce. The wine steward served Sonoma Cutter Chardonnay with the salad. Toni selected a medium well ribeye. The rest of the group followed suit except for Jelly who ordered rainbow trout. Dessert followed with champagne.

"How is the chocolate cake?" Julia asked Jelly.

"Oh great. Why don't you have a piece?"

"No, my cheesecake is too good to taste anything else right now."

"Well you know that I'll taste it, but just put it right here. The strawberries are great. They went overboard with the kiwi and peaches though. Oh Darius, the ice cream is homemade." Toni savored the sweet strawberries.

"Well, Julia, how's your marriage?" Darius somewhat smirked when he asked that question.

Julia half heard but joked around anyway, "What?" She followed Darius' eyes to see the 3-carat diamond solitaire and blinked. Toni noticed her gasping for air. Toni nudged Jelly who was talking a mile a minute. Julia still hadn't caught her breath.

"I asked you how is your marriage? The one that is upcoming as soon as you say yes and find a dress." Darius chuckled.

Julia finally took a breath. The tears rolled down her cheek. After she removed her hands from her mouth, she whispered, "Yes, yes, my marriage is fantastic."

"Congratulations. To the both of you. Toast. Toast. Please raise your glasses as I wish the two of you excellence in all that you do, happiness as a couple, as one. Please let me know when I need to buy my dress. I'm sure I'm a bridesmaid." Toni clinked her glass with Jelly's followed by a high five. One of her few crazy moments.

"Well Toni, you may not be a bridesmaid. Julia said that she always wanted an island wedding. My plan if she agrees is to do it after this weekend. We have some arrangements to make but the only major things are to get ourselves there and to send for anyone that she wants there. The only three people I need are already here."

"Are you serious?" Toni's eyes widened as if quarters needed to be inserted. "I'm there. I wouldn't miss nuptials for anything."

"Count us in." Martin spoke for himself and Jelly, who was still aghast with surprise.

The weekend passed so quickly that Toni cried only once when she thought of Philip. Toni felt as if she had lost several pounds. She missed Philip's company. The wedding reminded Toni of Philip's romantic nature. The loss deepened at moments like this. She remembered life changes for good reasons. Hers certainly had. The gorgeous blue water invoked memories of promises fulfilled with Philip.

"Their wedding was gorgeous. Surprising, but gorgeous. Darius has never kept anything from me like that before. Life is too short to allow nonsense to stop you from spending the rest of your life with the person that you love. I know that whatever time you spend is valuable and worthwhile."

"Well, Dr. T. we're glad that you're back. You seem to be doing well. All of the mail is at the corner of the desk. The checks are at the other corner." Jackie left Toni to read the other things that needed to be sent out. With Toni gone an extra couple of days, she was up against some deadlines.

Toni flipped through a couple of envelopes. She pulled a purple one from the collection. She knew it had to be from Jacque, her friend who moved north but still spoke with her frequently. She wiggled her finger between the flap and the other part of the envelope. Her excitement overcame her. She intended to take care of the envelope. She started again with her crystal-handled letter opener. Jackie usually did this for her. She wondered why this envelope had been left closed.

The lilac linen stationary released purple and gold confetti onto her desk. She read slowly, absorbing each word. She sensed Jacque's humor within each phrase.

Toni immediately responded to Jacque's letter.

Dear Jacque,

Thank you for your words of encouragement. I just returned from a vacation with the group. By the way, Darius and Julia are married. It was an island wedding. Too gorgeous. We traveled to Disneyworld, The Epcot Center, and Universal Studios. Orlando's heat reached an all time high. We spent ninety percent of our time thirsty.

Girl, I realize that life and love are so precious. We waste so much time worrying about the wrong things. I was incredibly blessed by Philip. It's simply awesome when someone's memories can still inspire and motivate you. Darius and Julia reminded me of each fulfilling moment we spent loving each other.

I had always asked for someone to love and someone to love me. Someone to whom I can give and give and give. I received him. We loved each other and we needed each other's warmth and spirituality. Sometimes at night I reach for him and as my hand passes over the sheets, I remember him as my best friend. I don't cry as much anymore. Holidays are hard though. I was looking forward to my birthday. It would have been my first birthday with him.

Since the wedding, I've spoken to my father on several occasions. He calls now. He had Philip help him see me. He hugged me like I was his little girl and I just melted. I plan to take him on a trip one day. But now we are just getting reacquainted. He's older and I'm certain that he doesn't want to grow any older without his children, at least not me. I'm not sure where his others are.

I've completely secured Philip's estate. The practice went to this young doctor from Dallas that had interned under Philip. Of course, Jackie takes all deliveries over there herself now.

I recently finished my manuscript. It is around 400 typed pages. I don't have an editor or anything yet. As a matter of fact, will you read it for me and tell me what you think? I wasn't really serious when I started. Though I did start a second one. When will *you be here again? My birthday is in two months so be sure to try and get here by then.*

Well Jacque, I hope all is well with you. I've got to finish reading this mail before Jackie kills me.

Call me when you get this so that I know that you got the book.

Mother and I are better, too. She supports and listens to me now. She doesn't have a copy of the book though.

Love Always, Toni.

The next envelope read Doubleday in the corner. "I wonder what they want."

Toni read out loud:

"When your assistant, Jackie, sent the first letter and outline, I almost threw it away. However, this unique approach earned you a phone call to Jackie at which time I asked her to send me the first few chapters. I called back and requested the rest. I finished reading it in two days.

"My favorite parts were the journal entries of the main character where she discovered the reality that love isn't always what we expect."

Toni remembered how hard it was to write certain parts. The main character and the man she met just began an affair that grew into a *Love Affair*. The damsel in distress discovered that the knight in shining armor existed only in her heart. But only until he decided to turn the affair around wore the heroine's dreams finally realized.

The letter closed instructing Toni to call immediately. The editor wanted to discuss the next steps. "Jackie, what should I do about this? What had you planned for the next move?"

Jackie's smirk gave her away, "Call, call now." She handed the letter back to Toni knowing she won. "That is, if you want this."

Another lifestyle change. Toni examined her hobby carefully as a profession, a lucrative and fascinating one. "Tracy Matthews please."

"Speaking."

"Tracy, this is Antoinette Harden-Morris. I just received your letter. I'm very excited." Toni looked up at Jackie, who was sitting at the edge of her seat.

"Mrs. Morris, when can you come to New York to discuss the details?"

"It will need to be a weekend. My clients are scheduled for three weeks solid. Any weekend is fine."

"I tell you what, I'll be there on Thursday. I'll meet you at 6:00 pm at the Four Seasons Hotel in the dining room."

"See you Thursday." Toni laid the phone on its cradle.

"Dr. T., you're going to be published!"

♦♦♦♦♦

Toni moved the staff meeting to her home. She extended the audience to include Darius, Julia, Jelly, Martin, and her family. Dinner started at 6:00 pm. By half past seven, dessert was served with coffee, tea, and champagne.

"Please raise your glass or mug with me. I have two announcements. The first one is I have signed a book deal. My first book, *Love Affair*, will be published by next February. I'll be on a promotional tour from January through April." Toni looked around at the shocked and surprised looks, as she waited to explain.

"It took about nine months to write and edit. Jackie sent it without my knowledge. But I have another story to share. So hold all that excitement until later. I still haven't told you guys about the honeymoon.

"The honeymoon was fabulous. The seven days and six nights we spent cruising through the mountains of Alaska were awesome. The days were warm. Nights were cool and passionate. Jaw-dropping scenery. Ice and snow, so intoxicating. We went on land twice. Alaskan culture was somewhat like it is depicted in *Northern Exposure*, yet more appealing. Philip snapped a picture of a moose on a hilltop. It's the picture on the lamp table in my office. Anyway, intimacy and closeness reached a distinct level only shared by soulmates. Although our love only lasted a few months, I haven't regretted our union. I have relished it. Nothing will match its magnitude. Lovers like us aren't made often. Perfect mates don't meet often enough. That's what Philip and I were: soulmates, best friends, and lovers. This emotional closeness intensified our passion and the act itself. At any rate, now I'll have a tangible lifetime memory of Philip. As usual, he didn't miss a detail. He left me with a child, his child, our child. I'm ten weeks. I love him, and I always will.

"He would be proud of the things that have transpired in my life since his death. I do wish he were here. Love like ours doesn't happen everyday. He kept all of his promises." She thought as she rubbed her tummy holding her unborn child, 'Now I have to keep all of mine.'

About the Author

Onedia Gage has authored several works including three books of poetry: The Blue Print, The Measure of a Woman, and In Purple Ink. Rev. Gage is an active member of The Church Without Walls/Brookhollow Baptist Church, and Zeta Phi Beta Sorority. She has two children. They like water and get there as often as possible.

www.ingramcontent.com/pod-product-compliance
Lightning Source LLC
Chambersburg PA
CBHW032046150426
43194CB00006B/435